THE CROSS OF CALVARY

THE CROSS OF CALVARY

Jessie Penn-Lewis

CLC
PUBLICATIONS
Fort Washington, PA 19034

The Cross of Calvary
Published by CLC Publications

U.S.A.
P.O. Box 1449, Fort Washington, PA 19034

UNITED KINGDOM
CLC International (UK)
Unit 5, Glendale Avenue, Sandycroft, Flintshire, CH5 2QP

Originally published by *The Overcomer Literature Trust*, England
This printing 2017

Printed in the United States of America

ISBN (paperback): 978-1-61958-292-7
ISBN (e-book): 978-1-61958-133-3

Unless otherwise noted, Scripture quotations are taken from the Holy Bible, American Standard Version, 1901.

Scripture quotations marked AV are from the Authorized (King James) Version, 1611.

Scripture quotations marked CH are from Conybeare and Howson's translation of the Epistles of St. Paul, 1852.

Italics in Scripture quotations are the emphasis of the author.

CONTENTS

CHAPTER ONE

"Behold the Lamb of God, which beareth the sin of the world."

—John 1:29, mg.

CALVARY AND THE FORESHADOWED CROSS

"And when they were come to the place, which is called Calvary, there they crucified him."

—Luke 23:33, A.V.

THE hour had come! The Lamb slain from the foundation of the world was now to be slain before the eyes of the world. "Herod and Pontius Pilate, with the Gentiles and the peoples of Israel, were gathered together, to do" what had been "foreordained to come to pass" (Acts 4:27–28).

By picture lessons and prophetic voices, for centuries before, God had been foretelling this dread hour; and He has been directing the world back to it for nearly two thousand years.

Calvary—which means "The Skull"—is the very pivot of the world's history. All prior things pointed forward to it; and all subsequent things point back to it. Even the future rests upon it, for the redeemed in heaven find it the center of heaven as they behold a Lamb in the midst of the throne, "standing as though it had been slain."

Seven hundred years before the Man Christ Jesus was led to the place called Calvary, a prophet inspired of God foreshadowed the cross and gave such a word-picture of the Saviour of the world that none but blinded hearts could fail to recognize Him when He came to earth—God manifest in the flesh.

Through the prophet Isaiah the Spirit of God poured a flood of light upon Calvary; depicting the pathway to the cross, its atoning sacrifice, its sufferings and its fruit—so all who knew the teachings of the book of Isaiah were without excuse as they crucified the Lord of glory.

The prophecy of Isaiah makes it clear that Christ was "delivered up by the determinate counsel and foreknowledge of God" (Acts 2:23), for God "foreshowed by the mouth of all the prophets, that His Christ should suffer" (Acts 3:18). And when at Calvary "lawless men did crucify and slay" the "Prince of Life," the rulers of Israel fulfilled the predictions of the prophets they read every sabbath day, by "condemning Him."

THE FORESHADOWED LAMB OF GOD (ISAIAH 53:1-3)

> "He hath no form nor comeliness. . . ."
>
> "No beauty that we should desire Him. . . ."
>
> "He was despised and forsaken of men . . . " (mg.).
>
> "A Man of sorrows, and acquainted with grief. . . ."
>
> "As one from whom men hide their face He was despised. . . ."

"Who hath believed that which we have heard?" (Isaiah 53:1, mg.) and "to whom hath the arm of Jehovah been revealed?" cries the prophet, who was reporting that which he had heard from God. But the message, or report, was so beyond all human thought, so contrary to all human ideas, that he wonders to whom the revelation will be given. For it was revealed to the old-time messengers of God that when they "testified beforehand the sufferings of Christ, and the glories that should follow them" (1 Peter 1:11–12), they were ministering to those who, in later years, would hear the message of the cross. And the apostle Peter writes that the Spirit of Christ Himself was in the prophets, testifying to the sufferings that would come to Him on earth. Isaiah foresees the questionings which would fill the minds of men as they heard the marvelous story of that which was told him from God seven hundred years before it came to pass. "Who hath believed?" and "to whom" is it revealed? he exclaims, as he describes the Christ growing up before the Father "as a tender plant; and as a root out of a dry ground." Very precious to God must have been the tender plant—the Branch that would "bear fruit" (Isaiah 11:1). For Israel, the choice vine, the plant of His delight (Isaiah 5:7, mg.), had disappointed the heavenly Husbandman and His cherished vineyard had become dry ground. But here was the Shoot out of a stock in Israel that would bring forth the fruit the Father wanted, although to the eyes of men there would be "no form nor comeliness," no beauty to cause them to desire Him.

He who was the precious, tender plant to the Father would be despised of men. He would be a "Man of sorrows, and acquainted with grief"; therefore they would reject and forsake Him, for suffering and sorrow are not attractive to men.

To Jehovah, His Righteous Servant would be "exalted and lifted up," even "very high," but to men He would be as one from whom they would hide their faces with astonishment, for His face and His form would be marred "more than the sons of men" (Isaiah 52:14).

How marred must have been the face of the Holy One of God from His crown of thorns! How lacerated the form of His sacred body from the scourging of the soldiers!—for the scourges were made from hundreds of leathern thongs, each armed at the point with an angular bony hook, or a sharp-edged cube (Krummacher).

"Look at yonder pillar, black with the blood of murderers and rebels. . . . Look at the rude and barbarous beings who busily surround their victim." See them "tear off His clothes, bind those hands, . . . press His gracious visage firmly against the shameful pillar," binding Him, "with ropes in such a manner that He cannot move or stir." See! The scourging lasts a full quarter of an hour! The scourges cut ever deeper into the wounds already made, and penetrate almost to the marrow until "His whole back appears an enormous wound" (Krummacher). A purple robe is then thrown over the form of the agonized Sufferer, and the twigs of a long-spiked thorn bush are twisted into a circle, and pressed upon His brow.

It was thus that His face was marred, and His form more than the sons of men. The prophet Isaiah had even foretold the words of the Man of sorrows, saying in His hour of agony, "I was not rebellious, neither turned away backward. I gave my back to the smiters, and My cheeks to them that plucked off the hair: I hid not My face from shame and spitting. For the Lord Jehovah will help Me . . . therefore have I set My face like a flint" (Isaiah 50:5–7).

Men hid their faces from Him, but "He hid as it were His face from us" is the marginal reading of the A.S.V. Did the group who had seen His face shine as the sun on the Mount of Transfiguration remember the hidden glory in that marred frame? Nay, even they "esteemed Him not" and forsook Him in His hour of shame.

The divine and human estimations of the Man of sorrows in His pathway to the cross are thus fully foreshadowed by the prophet, and the Holy Spirit as plainly foretells the substitutionary object of His death.

THE PURPOSE OF THE CROSS (VERSES 4–6)

> "He hath borne *our* griefs. . . ."
>
> "He hath carried *our* sorrows. . . ."
>
> "He was wounded for *our* transgressions. . . ."
>
> "He was bruised for *our* iniquities. . . ."
>
> "The chastisement of *our* peace was upon Him."

The Holy Spirit leaves no room for doubt as to the purpose and the cause of the sufferings of Christ. The word substitution is not actually used, but the language is unmistakably clear. This One with the marred face was bearing the "griefs" and "sorrows" of others. His wounds were for their transgressions, and the bruises upon His body were for their iniquities.

> "All we like sheep have gone astray; we have turned every one to his own way; and Jehovah hath made to light on Him the iniquity of us all" (verse 6, mg.).

Beholding, as it were, the One thus wounded and stricken—Isaiah knows not actually how—the prophet becomes a spokesman for the whole human race as he cries: "We behold His sufferings, we esteem Him stricken, smitten of God, and afflicted. We, who have gone astray! We, who have turned every one to his own way! But the Lord has laid upon Him—the Holy Son of our God—our iniquity, the iniquity of us all."

Thus briefly we have portrayed for us the result of the Fall in Eden and the cause and purpose of the cross.

Independence of God is the very essence of sin. To every man "his own way" ends in transgression and iniquity. The first *all* of verse 6 includes every human being brought into the world, and the second *all* proclaims the atoning sacrifice of Christ for every one under the curse of sin.

THE DEATH OF THE CROSS (VERSES 7-9)

> "He humbled Himself, and opened not His mouth. . . ."
>
> "A lamb that is led to the slaughter. . . ."
>
> "A sheep that before her shearers is dumb. . . ."
>
> "He was cut off out of the land of the living. . . ."
>
> "They made His grave with the wicked. . . ."

Isaiah now depicts the obedience unto death of the suffering one. He sees Him as a sheep in the hands of the shearers, dumb and passive; as a lamb being led to the slaughter, innocent and powerless. He who was equal with God counted it not a thing to be grasped, but emptied Himself and came in the likeness of men. As man He humbled Himself yet more, even unto death, consenting to be "led to the slaughter" as a victim in the hands of men.

How literally the prophecy was fulfilled in every detail the Gospels unfold.

The Christ standing before Pilate "when He was accused" answered nothing (Matthew 27:12), so that even the Governor marveled. From "oppression and judgment He was taken away" outside the city wall to the place called Calvary, and "as for His generation"—the people of His own nation and time—"who among them considered" the tragedy that was being enacted in their midst?

"Cut off out of the land of the living" in the very prime of life—how few realized that it was for the transgression of His people "to whom the stroke was due" (Isaiah 53:8).

How many in Jerusalem during that awful time "considered" and pondered over the Scripture of the prophets, which gave them the portrait of the Man they crucified? But the Man of sorrows knew! He said every step of His path must needs be "as it is written of Him." As He set His face to go on His last journey to Jerusalem, it was with the words "All the things that are written through the prophets shall be accomplished unto the Son of Man. For He shall be delivered up," "mocked," "shamefully treated," "spit upon," "and they shall scourge and kill Him" (Luke 18:31–33). He said, "It is written," when Judas betrayed Him, and when His disciples forsook Him; and again, after He was risen from the dead, He reminded them that when He was yet with them He had sought to prepare them for His cross by telling them of "all things that must needs be fulfilled"—revelations written in "the Law of Moses, and the Prophets, and the Psalms" (Luke 24:44), concerning Him.

Moreover, Isaiah not only foretold the sufferings and death of the Christ but the very way of His burial. His grave would be with the wicked, and He who had been despised and rejected of men would be "with a rich man in His death."

This was literally fulfilled; and the instrument prepared by God to carry out His counsels was found in "Joseph of Arimathea, a councillor of honorable estate," who was "looking for the kingdom of God" (Mark 15:43), and said to be a secret disciple of the Lord Jesus.

Joseph had sat in the council that condemned the Righteous One, but "he had not consented to their counsel and deed." He must have marveled with the Governor at the extraordinary silence of the Divine Sufferer, and in his heart re-echoed the verdict of Pilate that there was no cause worthy of death found in Him.

Unable to save the victim from His accusers, Joseph did what he could as soon as the sentence of death had been carried out by going boldly to Pilate and asking for the body of the Lord, then reverently laying it in his own new tomb.

THE PROVIDED LAMB OF GOD (VERSE 10)

> "It pleased Jehovah to bruise Him. . . ."
>
> "He hath put Him to grief. . . ."
>
> "His soul a guilt-offering [mg.] for sin. . . ."

"God will provide Himself a lamb," Abraham had said to Isaac on Mount Moriah, and Isaiah foreshadows the Lamb provided by God Himself, to be revealed in the fullness of time.

Despised and rejected by men, wounded, bruised, cut off out of the land of the living, this One with the marred face is now plainly described as "a guilt-offering for sin"—the antitype of all the guilt-offerings sacrificed day by day in Israel, by the command of God Himself. Hitherto the worshipers had to bring the sacrifice, but when God provided the Lamb, and laid upon Him the iniquity of all, there would be nought for them to do but accept the provision made for them. The One who had grown up before the Father as a "tender plant" is "put to grief" by the express will of Jehovah. It was His sovereign pleasure to "bruise Him." In this passage we see Calvary from the standpoint of the Father, who so loved the world that He spared not His own Son but delivered Him up for us all; just as in the preceding paragraph we have foretold the voluntary offering of the Son, when "He humbled Himself" and gave Himself up to death as a "lamb led to the slaughter," a sheep in the hands of the shearers, opening not His mouth.

THE FRUIT OF THE CROSS (VERSES 10–11)

"He shall see His seed. . . ."

"He shall prolong His days. . . ."

"He shall see of the travail of His soul. . . ."

"He shall . . . be satisfied. . . ."

Another aspect of the cross is referred to in these words. Calvary is viewed now as in harmony with a law of God—the law of sacrifice for fruitfulness.

Bruised and put to grief, the Christ is said to "prolong His days" through the seed thus brought into being, and "the pleasure of the Lord" in seeking fruit after His own image prospers in His hand.

The yearning of the Creator for fellowship with beings created after His own likeness is one of the greatest mysteries in the revelation of the heart and character of Jehovah. "Let Us make man in Our image, after Our likeness" (Genesis 1:26), the Triune God had said, when the beautiful earth, created by His word, lay before Him, but with no beings upon it answering to His heart.

"He shall see His seed." "He shall see and be satisfied with the travail of His soul" (mg.) reveals the same yearning in the heart of the God-Man. Grieved over the fall of the first creation, He gives His life on Calvary for the birth of a new race, a re-creation of those who had gone astray and turned each one to "his own way." By His death "making many righteous" through His bearing of their iniquities, He beholds the fruit of His travail and is satisfied.

This new birth for the fallen children of the first Adam is declared to be the fruit of His cross by the Lord Jesus Himself, shortly after the beginning of His public ministry, when He told Nicodemus that sinful men "must" be born again, and that the Son of Man "must" be "lifted up" (John 3:14–16) to become the source of life eternal to them.

THE VICTORY OF THE CROSS (VERSE 12)

> "Therefore will I divide Him a portion with the great. . . ."
>
> "He shall divide the spoil with the strong. . . ."

Yet another aspect of Calvary is shown us here. Another person, called the "strong," is mentioned, and the language used suggests a battle and the dividing of the "spoil" won in the fight. Elsewhere Isaiah speaks of the "prey of the terrible" and the deliverance of the "captives of the just" from the "mighty" (Isaiah 49:24–25, mg.).

It is also said that the spoil is given to the Man of sorrows "because He poured out His soul unto death," and "because He . . . was numbered with the transgressors."

Calvary was thus to be not only the bearing of our iniquities that we might be healed; not merely the guilt-offering for sin through which we would be made righteous; not just a travail for the birth of a new race in the likeness of the Son of God. It was also a battle with a terrible foe—for the deliverance of those held captive by his power. This accords with other passages of Scripture, for David in vision beheld the ascended Lord leading "captivity captive" into the sanctuary on high, and the inspired writer of the Epistle to the Hebrews, says that "through death" the Christ brought to nought the devil, that He might "deliver all them who through fear of death were all their lifetime subject to bondage" (Hebrews 2:15).

It is written that He took the spoil from the strong because He was "numbered with the transgressors." In perfect obedience to His Father's will, He accepted and drank the cup of suffering and death! How can we fathom what it meant to Him "who knew no sin" to be numbered with the transgressors" and "made sin on our behalf" (2 Corinthians 5:21)? This view of Calvary may reveal to us one cause of the victory of Christ over the terrible one. The devil had sought to be exalted even as the Most High, but the Son of God humbled Himself and consented to be made lower than the lowest. Therefore God highly exalted Him, and gave unto Him the Name which is above every name; for Calvary in its depth of shame on earth was exaltation in heaven.

THE EFFECT OF THE CROSS IN HEAVEN (VERSE 12)

> "He bare the sin of many and made intercession for the transgressors."

In this brief sentence we are given a glimpse into the heavens to see the Victor from Calvary within the veil, "before the face of God" (Hebrews 9:24) on behalf of all for whom He died.

"Numbered with the transgressors," He could make intercession for the transgressors; for He was "touched with the feeling" of their sorrows, having been Himself tempted in all points like as they (yet without sin). For prior to the cross He "suffered being tempted" (Hebrews 2:18) when He walked on earth as man.

Let us go to Calvary, and in the light thrown on it by the prophecy of Isaiah, behold Him who for the joy set before Him endured the cross, despising the shame. The hour had come for which he had entered into this world. Hear the God-Man cry "It is finished," as He bows His head and yields up His spirit into His Father's hand! We know now that He is the Father's provided Lamb, the guilt-offering for sin—the One who with a visage more marred than any man's was wounded and bruised for our iniquities, so that by His stripes we may be healed.

Sometime later, after the day of Pentecost had fully come, a man of authority was riding in his chariot in the desert, reading aloud the prophecy of Isaiah. At the moment he reached the words "He was led as a sheep to the slaughter . . . His life is taken from the earth," a certain disciple named Philip drew nigh, and was bidden of the Holy Spirit to run over to the chariot. Sitting beside the eunuch, he preached unto him JESUS from the prophecy of Isaiah.

The Spirit-given foreshadowing of the cross was now the Spirit-given message to a seeking heart through a messenger instructed by Him (see Acts 8:26–35).

Thus did the Holy Spirit bear witness that Isaiah had truly foreshown the Christ of God, and that

> "He saw His glory, and he spake of Him" (John 12:41).

CHAPTER 2

"The Spirit of Truth . . . shall glorify Me: for He shall take of Mine, and shall declare it unto you."

—John 16:13–14.

THE CROSS INTERPRETED BY THE ASCENDED CHRIST

"The gospel which was preached by me . . . is not after man. For neither did I receive it from man, nor was I taught it, but it came to me through revelation of Jesus Christ."

—Galatians 1:11–12.

WE have already noticed the teaching of the apostle Peter that the Spirit of Christ indwelt and controlled the old-time prophets when they testified beforehand about the sufferings of Christ and the glories that would follow.

This Spirit-testimony not only revealed the Son of God as suffering the death on the cross when His hour had come, but, in the broadest sense, set forth Christ as being the theme of prophecy from the beginning of the world. By the Holy Spirit He inspired the preaching of His coming sacrificial death during the centuries preceding His manifestation to the world. Since this was the case before His passion, there is no reason to think that after He ascended into heaven He then committed the interpretation and proclamation of His crucifixion entirely to the wisdom of men.

The apostles were eyewitness of His sufferings, but they were not left to preach what each may have thought to be the meaning of the cross, for we find that in the upper room on the Day of Pentecost the Third Person of the blessed Trinity—the Spirit of Truth who proceeds from the Father—takes possession of the chosen band of witnesses to equip them for their work.

The Holy Spirit, the gift of the Father to the Son for His redeemed on earth, comes forth Himself to bear testimony to the Crucified One and, through His disciples, to witness to His death and rising again.

"Ye shall receive upon you the power of the Holy Spirit, and ye shall be witnesses unto Me," the risen Lord had declared. And now, energized by the Holy Spirit, we find these chosen witnesses bearing testimony to the death and resurrection of the Lord Jesus.

"Ye . . . did crucify and slay," but "God raised up" (Acts 2:23–24). "God hath made Him both Lord and Christ, this Jesus whom ye crucified" (Acts 2:36). "Ye denied the Holy and Righteous One, and asked for a murderer to be granted unto you, and killed the Prince of Life; whom God raised from the dead" (Acts 3:14–15).

"You crucified the one whom God has raised." This was the burden of the message borne witness to by "distributions of the Holy Spirit," and by signs and wonders done through the name of the crucified and risen Son of God.

Stephen in particular, "full of grace and power, wrought great wonders and signs among the people," bearing witness before the Jewish council to the crucified Jesus, and then crowning his testimony by laying down his life for the One who had died for him.

The fruit of the cross was manifested in a signal way through the death of Stephen, for from his death sprang the one who was to proclaim in mighty powers the full meaning of the sacrifice of the Son of God.

In the death of Stephen and the resulting conversion of Saul the Pharisee we have an object lesson of the way in which the message of the cross is the power of God. We learn that it is the *word* of the cross, spoken by the Holy Spirit in conjunction with the *spirit* of the cross imparted to the messenger, that produces the *fruit* of the cross in other souls. It may even be said that Saul the Pharisee was an eyewitness of the sufferings of the Lord Jesus in His martyr Stephen, for he heard the dying Stephen pray, "Lord, lay not this sin to their charge"—just as the Lord had prayed on the cross for those who crucified Him, saying, "Father, forgive them, for they know not what they do."

We may well believe that an arrow of conviction pierced the heart of Saul that day, and when he so suddenly met the risen Lord on the way to Damascus and heard him say, "Saul, Saul, why persecutest thou Me? It is hard for thee to kick against the pricks," Saul knew that he had seen the Spirit of Christ in the martyr Stephen . . . and the "chosen vessel" was won to the feet of his Lord.

Isaiah the prophet had been chosen and fitted by God to foreshadow the wondrous story of the cross and portray in tender language the characteristics of the Lamb of God. Even so was Paul chosen by the Lord to receive and proclaim the message of the cross. Isaiah and Paul were each prepared for their special service by a personal meeting with God—a meeting which aroused in each such self-abhorrence that Isaiah could but cry, "Woe is me, for I am undone," and the apostle say, "In me . . . dwelleth no good thing." Each also came to the same entire surrender to God, Isaiah saying, "Here am I, send me," and Paul, "Lord, what wilt Thou have me to do?"

"Isaiah's bitter weeping over his people" (Isaiah 22:4) and Paul's agony of soul over the blindness of Israel (Romans 9:3) also show that both were men capable of deep suffering and of utter abandonment to the service of God, and that both had largeness of spirit to receive and communicate the teachings of the Spirit of God. Each was given the theme of Calvary, the one in its germ and the other in its full fruition. Each was inspired by the Spirit of Christ Himself—in the one, testifying beforehand of His sufferings, and in the other, interpreting the glorious results of His death.

We are not surprised, therefore, to find Paul declaring emphatically that the gospel which he preached was "not after man" nor did he "receive it from man"—not even from one who had been an eyewitness of the sufferings of Christ; that he was not taught it by anyone, but that it had been given to him by direct "revelation of Jesus Christ." And so he wrote to the Galatians, "The message you have heard from me was out and out divine, authentic from the throne. . . . The risen Lord personally unveiled it to me" (paraphrase outline of Galatians 1:11–24, Moule).

We have then this wonderful and solemn fact, that the risen and ascended Lord, with the marks of His passion upon the sacred body He carried into heaven, *Himself* interpreted to Paul the object of His death. If we keep this in mind as we meditate upon the message of Calvary as expressed in the writings of Paul, the "word of the cross" will in truth be unto us the "energy of God." That the gospel of the cross as preached by Paul was given him directly by the Lord Himself is also proved by the results of his visit to the leading apostles of Christ in Jerusalem. "By revelation" (Galatians 2:2) Paul is bidden to lay before the apostles the gospel he was preaching among the Gentiles, and when he did this he found that he had been taught so fully by the risen Lord Himself that they who had seen Christ die, had held converse with Him after He was risen from the dead, and had been filled with the Holy Spirit on the day of Pentecost, had nothing to impart to the one chosen of the Lord to proclaim the message of His love.

Not only had they nothing to impart, but they "perceived the grace given unto him," and acknowledged that this man had in truth been "entrusted with the gospel" (Galatians 2:6–9). Accordingly they gave unto him the "right hand of fellowship," proving for all time that the gospel preached by him was in full harmony with the gospel proclaimed by all the apostles—the gospel doubtless given to them by Christ Himself when after His passion He appeared unto them "by the space of forty days," "speaking the things concerning the kingdom of God" (Acts 1:3).

Since the message of Calvary was therefore given to Paul by direct revelation of the Lord, we do not marvel that it dominated his life and was woven into the very texture of all his writings. Burnt into his heart, he who had not seen the God-Man actually die[1] preached His cross and passion with such intensity and such manifest illumination of the Holy Spirit that he could declare to the Galatians that "Jesus Christ had been painted large upon His cross to their very eyes" (translation of Galatians 3:1, Moule).

May God the Holy Spirit bear witness again to the gospel of the cross through Paul as we reverently listen to the Lord Himself, through His messenger, interpreting His death.

THE CROSS TO THE NATURAL MAN

> "The natural man receiveth not the things of the Spirit . . . they are foolishness unto him."—1 Corinthians 2:14.
>
> "The word of the cross is to them that are perishing foolishness."—1 Corinthians 1:18.
>
> "Christ crucified, unto Jews a stumbling-block, and unto Gentiles foolishness."—1 Corinthians 1:23.

Although Paul received his gospel by direct revelation of Jesus Christ, he was under no delusion as to its reception by the natural man. Like Isaiah he knew that the cross as the "arm of the Lord" must be revealed by the Holy Spirit, for to the darkened intellect (Ephesians 4:18) and rebellious will of the children of unbelief, the whole message would appear but folly.

"Salvation through the death of another? It is contrary to all justice! Man unable to save himself? No, it is all folly!"

To the Jews the word of the cross would be a still greater stumbling block. Was it not written in their Scriptures, "He that is hanged is accursed in the sight of God" (Septuagint)?

Again and again Paul must have had the words cast in his teeth, "accursed of God," or "an insult to God," as he preached to the Jews a crucified Messiah, for in speaking of the Lord Jesus they often called Him by the name "the gibbetted one," which they found in the original Hebrew of Deuteronomy 21:23 (Lightfoot).

Apart from the illumination of the Spirit, the Jews could not see that the very words in Deuter-onomy *interpreted* the cross of Christ, who became a "curse for *us*" on the tree of Calvary.

But the Jews were looking for a Messiah who would reign as a King on earth, and in reading the prophecy of Isaiah they had only seen foreshadowings of glory and kingship in the Coming One. With preconceived ideas as to the tokens of authority which would make known unto them their looked-for Messiah, the Jews had demanded of the Lord Jesus again and again to "show us a sign from heaven," and with pain the Lord had replied, "There shall no sign be given" but "the sign of Jonah." "For as Jonah . . . so shall the Son of Man be . . . in the heart of the earth" (Matthew 12:38–40).

Calvary and the grave, foretold by the prophet Isaiah and pictured again in the mysterious experience of Jonah the prophet, was the special "sign" promised by God to make known the Messiah, but Isaiah had written of Israel, "their ears are dull of hearing, and their eyes they have closed" (Matthew 13:14–16), and his prophecy concerning the blinded people was fulfilled.

"The Jews ask for signs," writes Paul, but have not eyes to see the signs foretold by God; the "Greeks seek after wisdom," and fail to perceive that "Christ crucified" is the power and wisdom of God.

THE CROSS AND HUMAN WISDOM

> "The word of the cross . . . is the power of God. For it is written, I will destroy the wisdom of the wise."—1 Corinthians 1:18–19.

Paul, who had himself once been a Pharisee rejecting with bitter antagonism the story of a crucified Messiah, with heaven-lit vision sees deeply into the purpose of the cross. He beholds it as the master-stroke of Jehovah against one cause of the Fall in Eden.

"The woman saw that the tree . . . was to be desired to make one wise" (Genesis 3:6).

The desire of knowledge beyond the limit set by the Lord was one of the causes of the Fall, the effect thereof continuing unto this day, for pride of intellect is still a barrier between men and the knowledge of their Creator.

Salvation through the cross was a master-stroke of the All-wise Creator against the pride of knowledge in His fallen creatures, for the "word of the cross" is the power of God to "destroy" or bring to nought "the wisdom of the wise." The cross as the power of God is so wholly beyond the comprehension of the natural man that he must submit his intellect to his Creator and accept the message on the word of Jehovah alone.

"The foolishness of God is wiser than men," says the Scripture, and in the day when all men shall know themselves as they are known by their Creator, all that appeared to carnal reasoning as "foolishness" will be proved to be the highest wisdom of God.

The "word of the cross" is the energy of God and through it the All-wise Lord is already making "foolish" the "wisdom of the world"; for while the world "through its wisdom" is failing utterly to know Him, it is "God's good pleasure through the foolishness of the thing preached" (1 Corinthians 1:21, mg.) to "save them that believe." Through the "thing preached" which is accounted foolishness, God is working the miracle of salvation from the guilt and power of sin and re-creating a new race after the likeness of Him who is the Firstborn of many brethren—the Firstborn from the dead.

The "weakness of God" manifested in Him who was "crucified through weakness" is "stronger than men." The weak and suffering Saviour upon His cross of shame is mighty to save all who believe in Him.

THE CROSS AND TRUE WISDOM

> "Howbeit we speak wisdom . . . yet a wisdom not of this world. . . . We speak God's wisdom in a mystery."—1 Corinthians 2:6–8.

The word of the cross, unto those who are "being saved," is the power of God to bring to nought the pride of knowledge so that they may be taught God's wisdom: "things which eyes saw not, and ears heard not, and which entered not into the heart of man."

It is a wisdom which is a mystery to the natural man, but which is revealed by the Spirit of God unto all those who love God; a wisdom, writes the apostle, which will be "unto our glory" when the wisdom of this world shall have passed away.

"God's wisdom in a mystery" is "the mystery of God, even Christ, in whom are all the treasures of wisdom and knowledge hidden" (Colossians 2:2–3). A Messiah crucified is unto the called, both Jews and Greeks, the power of God and the wisdom of God (1 Corinthians 1:23–24, mg.).

CHAPTER 3

"Forasmuch then as Christ suffered . . . arm ye yourselves with the same thought: for he that hath suffered in the flesh hath ceased from sin."

—1 Peter 4:1, mg.

THE TWOFOLD MESSAGE OF THE CROSS

"Having made peace through the blood of His cross . . . you . . . hath he reconciled in the body of His flesh through death."

—Colossians 1:20–22.

THE prophecy of Isaiah tells us that the sufferings and death of the Man of Sorrows were not for Himself but for those who had gone astray: "an offering for sin" by the express will of the Father, who was pleased to "bruise Him" and "put Him to grief."

Paul the apostle takes up the same theme and writes to the Romans that God Himself purposed the sacrifice of Christ Jesus to be "a propitiation through faith in His blood" (Romans 3:25), for only thus could He "pass over sin" and show His righteousness to a guilty world.

Jehovah spared not His own Son, but delivered Him up for us all! Yea, it is written that God Himself "was in Christ, reconciling the world unto Himself," for Father and Son are One.

Heralds sent forth and equipped by God the Holy Spirit must proclaim the tidings of peace. Commissioned by the risen Son of God as His ambassadors, they are to plead on "behalf of Christ" with perishing souls, and "as though God were entreating" by them they are to say, "Be ye reconciled to God."

To the Colossians, Paul writes, "Having made peace through the blood of His cross" you—who were separated from God, and enemies *to* God, because of your evil doings—"you . . . now hath He reconciled in the body of His flesh through death" (1:20–22).

"Having made peace through the blood of His cross" refers to the propitiatory aspect of the sacrifice of Christ when He trod the winepress alone, and of the people there were none with Him (Isaiah 63:3, A.V.). However, the reconciliation of the sinner to God "in the body of His flesh through death" shows us the Saviour and the saved becoming as *one*. In this latter aspect we see the second Adam as the Representative Man, and discern how, in His death, all who are united to Him by faith have suffered the penalty of their sins and are reconciled to God through Him.

"In the body of His flesh through death, [His intent is] to present you holy and without blemish and unreprovable before Him," continues the apostle.

The cross is the gateway through which the reconciled soul passes into the new sphere where it is presented in Christ to the Father as "holy and without blemish and unreprovable before Him." Those who are thus reconciled *die* with Christ to their old sins. Their "evil works," which made them alienated and enemies to God in their mind, are now left behind. They are *not* reconciled to continue in the life they lived *before*.

The message of "peace through the blood of His cross" and reconciliation to God in the body of Christ through death, therefore, includes deliverance from the *power* as well as the *guilt* of sin.

In still plainer language does the apostle Peter proclaim the deliverance from the bondage of sin in linkage with the remission of past sins. Writing in his First Epistle about the sufferings of Christ, he says, "His own self bare our sins in His body upon the tree, that we, having died unto sins, might live unto *righteousness*" (1 Peter 2:24). The alternative reading given in the margin of the A.S.V. is still more striking, for it says that Christ "*carried up* our sins in His body to the tree"—surely not that we might continue under their control and do them again and again!

The union of the believer with his Saviour in death is thus clearly expressed by the apostle. Having made peace by the atoning sacrifice of His cross, the Lord Jesus carried our sins to the tree so that in Him we have died to them and their power—and now, sharing His *life* from God, we may "live unto righteousness" by the might of the Holy and Righteous One who dwells within our hearts.

"By whose stripes ye were healed" adds the apostle, quoting the prophecy of Isaiah, and linking the deliverance from the guilt and bondage of sin to that most sacred foreshadowing of the cross. It was the Lamb of God who had the actual bruising and suffering on our behalf, and this was so that the *healing* power of His life might be imparted to us. We who believe that He has carried our sins to the tree, and in Him have died unto those sins, are henceforth to live unto God.

This is the message of Calvary as revealed unto Paul by the risen Lord, and by the words of Peter confirmed as the gospel preached by all the apostles in the days since Pentecost. Incalculable loss has come to the Church of God by the frequent severance of these two aspects of the "word of the cross" in its proclamation of the gospel of Calvary.

Moreover, deliverance from the power of sin was manifestly not taught by Paul as an "advanced" experience, for when he wrote to the converts in Rome he seemed to speak of our death with Christ as an elementary stage of experience—ignorance of which surprised him—for their fellowship with Christ's death was the *only* basis upon which they could realize the newness of life in Him.

THE CROSS AND THE BONDAGE OF SIN

> "Crucified with Him . . . that so we should no longer be in bondage to sin."—Romans 6:6.

"Reconciled to God through the death of His Son, much more, being reconciled, shall we be saved in His life" (Romans 5:10, mg.), writes Paul to the Romans, as he goes on to show the wondrous plan of God, that all who are thus reconciled and recipients of the gift of righteousness should "reign in life" (Romans 5:17). As sin had once reigned over them, even so might grace reign through Jesus Christ.

But someone may raise the question, "Should we not then continue in sin so that God may show more of His abounding grace?" (see Romans 6:1). "God forbid!" bursts forth the apostle. The death of Christ, and the free grace of God abounding therefrom, can *never* be meant to minister to sin! It is true that God's abounding grace is given to sinners through the death of His Son, but with the Son of God we "died." Then how shall we who have died to sin live any longer therein? (Romans 6:2).

The apostle of the Cross is deeply moved as he writes! By "revelation of Jesus Christ" he had been shown the meaning of Calvary, and in the light of the cross had seen the depth of the Fall and the exceeding sinfulness of sin—which demanded nothing less than the death of the Son of God Himself, in unparalleled suffering and shame, to rescue the doomed sinner.

"*Continue* in sin" when Christ had died to deliver from sin? God forbid! Sin has abounded, but "grace did abound more exceedingly" to save the sinner from his bonds.

In the light shining upon Calvary as unveiled to him by Christ, the apostle shows the meaning of that death so that none in Rome could be ignorant any longer of the purpose for which Christ died.

"Our old man was crucified with Him" is the message of Calvary to the fallen sinner, and is the secret of deliverance from the bondage of sin. All who were baptized into Christ "were baptized into His death." Through "baptism into death" they were buried into His grave for the express purpose "that like as Christ was raised from the dead" (Romans 6:4), they might look upon His cross and grave as a great gulf fixed between them and their past, and with the *risen* Christ emerge to "walk in newness of life" (Romans 6:4).

This, of course, was if they were really and intimately united with the Lord in His death! A mental assent alone would not produce a real union with the risen Lord. They must by the Holy Spirit be so vitally united with the crucified One that they shared the very "likeness" of His death (Romans 6:5).

And if this union existed, then they would realize the power of His resurrection and know that they were "crucified with Him." So they would "no longer be in bondage to sin"—slaves of sin—for "he that hath died is justified from sin" (Romans 6:6–7). Sin has no longer a claim to reign—its tyranny is over.

Moreover, the death of Christ meant more than negative deliverance. They were set free from the reign of sin not only by *death* but by *life*. The life of Christ which triumphed over death and the grave would be manifested in them; for if they truly "died" to the old they would live with Christ and share the life that He now lives—a new life, a life "unto God" (Romans 6:10).

Abundant life—a reigning in life—was the purpose of Calvary. The death Christ died He died unto sin for *us*, and He died "once for all" (Romans 6:10, mg.).

So they were to *reckon* themselves dead unto sin with Him and utterly refuse to let it reign over them, for they were "alive unto God in Christ Jesus." Abiding in Him as their very life, they would *reign* in life in Jesus Christ their Lord.

But they must not forget that this must be lived out in practice! They cannot be truly crucified with Christ and at the same time yield to sin or hand over the members of their body as instruments of unrighteousness, or else they would be making "void the grace of God." If they desired to realize the full deliverance of Calvary, they must not only gladly recognize their death with the Crucified One but they must present themselves unto God as "men living after death"

(Romans 6:13, Moule), and in "newness of life" yield the members of their bodies unto God as weapons of righteousness.

But another question arises here. Will not the grace that sets us free bring in a danger of license beyond the bounds of liberty? (Romans 6:15).

"God forbid!" again cries the apostle. Did they not know that the change brought about by union with Christ in His death and resurrection meant a *revolution* deep down in the center of a man's being? That those who had thus proved the power of Christ's death became "obedient from the heart" to that pattern whereunto they "were delivered" (Romans 6:17, mg.)? In newness of life, true believers gladly became "servants of God" instead of servants to sin, and of their own free choice chose day by day to present their bodies as "bondservants of righteousness" in joyous obedience unto God.

In this chapter in Romans the severing power of the cross is clearly seen. The work of deliverance from the guilt and bondage of sin was accomplished at Calvary, and the apostle calls upon the Roman Christians to enter upon the fruit of Christ's death by a decisive act of faith. With Christ upon the cross they *died*, and in His death they were *cut off* from their old life. "United with Him by the likeness of His death," they were to account themselves crucified *with* Him, "dead indeed unto sin" (Romans 6:11, A.V.), and living unto God in Him.

"But I have reckoned thus, and it seems nothing but reckoning a *lie*!" cries some longing heart.

Ah, soul, maybe your eyes are in the wrong direction. You are looking within, occupied more with your "reckoning" than with the work of your Saviour. The Holy Spirit will not bear witness to your "reckon" apart from the *object* of your reckoning. Look away to *Calvary*. The Lord Jesus died on your behalf, and as your Representative carried you with Him to His cross. Are you honestly determined to part with every known sin, and willing for the death with Christ to be made practical in your experience? Then from this crucial moment see yourself as nailed to the tree with your crucified Lord.

Relying upon the Holy Spirit, and in *faith* in the word of God, "let not sin therefore reign," for God has said that through Christ's death and your sharing of that death "sin shall not have the mastery over you" (Romans 6:14, C.H.).

Hidden in Christ upon His cross and joined to Him in His life, your part, O child of God, is the continual choice of your will—for "to whom ye yield," his "servants ye are" (Romans 6:16, A.V.). In the hour of sore temptation, in the center of your being you must promptly retire, so to speak, to the cross, and, hiding in Him who carried you there, refuse to be drawn out of your place in Him. Do not struggle with anything that comes to you, but hand over all to Him whose life you *do* share, and you shall find that He is able to deliver and to keep you day by day.

"But now, being freed from the bondage of sin, and enslaved to the service of God" (Romans 6:22, C.H.), you must deal honestly with sin, calling sin, *sin.* Be steadfastly purposed to walk in obedience to your Lord, counting upon Him to work in you to will and to do of His good pleasure.

Let every stress of trial or temptation drive you to the searchlight of His face that you may see all things in *His* light. So shall you "walk in the light as He is in the light," with the precious blood of Jesus Christ cleansing you from all sin. "And if any man sin, we have an Advocate with the Father, Jesus Christ the Righteous"—He who is "the propitiation for our sins; and not for ours only, but also for the whole world" (1 John 2:1–2).

But before we crave deliverance we must necessarily feel the weight of our chains. At this point we come to the *purpose of the law*, unfolded in the seventh chapter of Romans.

CHAPTER 4

"Faithful is the saying: For if we died with Him, we shall also live with Him."

—2 Timothy 2:11.

THE CROSS AND THE LAW

"Ye also were made dead to the law through the body of Christ. . . . now we have been discharged from the law, having died to that wherein we were holden."

—Romans 7:4–6.

DELIVERANCE through death is still the message of the apostle. The cross of Calvary is the place of reconciliation with God and of freedom from the power of sin, but he who is crucified with Christ dies with Him not only to the bondage of sin but to the bondage of the "*law*," which demanded from a helpless sinner an obedience it could not get and brought him deeper and deeper into the powerlessness of death.

The apostle's trend of thought in Romans 5, 6, 7 and 8 is marvelously in accord with the facts of actual experience in the Christian life. In fact, this group of chapters can only be clearly understood *from the inside*—that is, by having in some measure passed through these stages of experience, so as to be able to see things from the standpoint of Paul as he wrote to the Roman Christians.

"The law came in" he writes, "*that the trespass might abound*" (Romans 5:20–21). But God only purposed to reveal the "abounding" of the sin and its heinousness so that His *grace* might be shown to "abound *more exceedingly*."

That "as *sin reigned*" (Romans 5:20–21) over the poor sinner, even so might "*grace*"—the free gift of righteousness—"*reign*" and triumph in the redeemed man.

The way that grace might come in and reign is then shown to be by *death*, for nothing but death could release the sinner from his chains. The wages of sin is death. The penalty of sin *must* be paid; the verdict of death *must* be carried out. And in the death of Christ as the Representative Man the penalty *was* carried out, and the reign of sin *ends* in all who have died with their crucified Lord.

The believer also dies to the *law* which condemned him to death. United to Christ in His death, he is "*made dead to the law through the body of Christ*" (Romans 7:4), and is therefore "*discharged*" from the claims of the law, "*having died*" to that which held him in bondage.

The law can no longer say to one who has died, "Thou shalt," for he has passed through the gateway of death to another sphere, where the law cannot follow him—a sphere "*in Christ Jesus*," wherein he serves God in a new way, with a new spirit of glad obedience to the letter of the law (Romans 7:6).

Another question occurs at this point: *Are we then to say that the "law" given by God is sin?* (cf. Romans 7:7). Once more the apostle answers "*God forbid!*" and proceeds to show the reason why the law was given and the practical working of the law in bringing the soul to the place where he is *ready* to be delivered by the crucified and risen Lord. For the message of deliverance through death with Christ comes as glad tidings only to those who are at an *end* of themselves. The law is our *schoolmaster*, to bring us to Christ.

After speaking of the discharge from the claims of the law, the apostle breaks out into vivid description of the bitter conflict in the soul of the one who delights in the will of God in his inward man but has failed to yet *apprehend* this deliverance through the death of Christ which Paul has been describing.

Whatever primary object Paul may have had in mind when he wrote the much-debated seventh chapter of Romans, at least we may safely say that it is a powerful picture of a man under the tyranny of sin who is roused to activity by his desire to fulfill the will of God.

It is the *law* that brings the soul to the place of death, for "death" is simply a cessation from struggling—the point at which the soul arrives when it can battle no more and cries in despair, "Who shall deliver me?" "*I through the law died unto the law*," writes Paul, "that I might live unto God" (Galatians 2:19). It is easy to discuss the seventh chapter of Romans from the academic point of view, but if we set ourselves in earnest to break our own bonds we will soon learn the reality of the picture and the bitterness of the experience it describes.

Let us look briefly at the passage and see how the law works in bringing souls to an end of themselves, ready to be delivered by Jesus Christ our Lord.

THE LAW WAS GIVEN TO MAKE US KNOW WHAT SIN IS

> "I had not known sin, except through the law."—Verse 7.

For instance, unless God had given a law and said, "Thou shalt not covet," how could we know that to covet was a sin?

THE LAW WAS GIVEN TO SHOW THE ANTAGONISM OF SIN

> "Sin, finding occasion, wrought in me . . . coveting: for apart from the law sin is dead."—Verse 8.

How actually true in every human heart the picture is! If we are told not to covet, we find ourselves doing at once the very thing we are forbidden to do. "*Thou shalt not*" arouses against the holy will of God all the antagonism that is in fallen human nature, for "*the mind of the flesh is enmity against God*" (Romans 8:7).

Apart from the commands of the law "*sin is dead*," i.e., there is no antagonism or fight. Let men go their own way and fulfill the desires of their flesh and of their mind and there is no battle; but let them come face to face with the law of God and *try to obey it*, then sin rouses up and works all manner of things in them contrary to the commandment of God.

The law is therefore given to *show the man himself* the antagonism that is within him to the law of God.

THE LAW WAS GIVEN TO BRING US TO DEATH

> "I was alive apart from the law once: but when the commandment came, sin revived, and I died."—Verse 9.

Once upon a time I knew nothing of the claims of God, "*I was alive*, apart from the law."

I thought all was well—but suddenly I came face to face with the "*Thou shalt*" and "*Thou shalt not*" of my Creator. Something within me woke up and fought against God's law; "*sin revived*" where it had been dormant. I found I could not obey the law, for I was helpless.

Yes, sin took its opportunity and asserted its power and claim upon me *through the very commandment of God*. I found it actually stronger than myself. It *beguiled* me! I had to yield to its temptations, even while knowing the consequences to be death. So to speak, sin "*slew me*" (v. 11) by showing me that I had nothing before me but the wages of sin—death.

God's commandment should have led me to live a better life, but instead it made me sink deeper into the helplessness of death (v. 10), and in hopeless despair, "*I died*."

THE LAW WAS GIVEN TO SHOW THE SINFULNESS OF SIN

> "The law is holy . . . righteous, and good. But sin, . . . shown to be sin, . . . through the commandment [became] exceeding sinful."—Verses 12–13.

"Sin . . . *shown to be sin*" by the holiness of the law! How wonderful is the plan devised by the Creator to teach the creature—who has no conception of sin—*what sin is*, and still more to make him know his need of salvation. Sin must become "exceeding sinful" before it is loathed—before one's desire is aroused to have it put away and deliverance known from its bonds.

The *need* of a Saviour must be felt before the Saviour Himself can be welcomed.

The *depth* of one's fall must be seen or else the height, and depth, and breadth, and length of salvation cannot be understood.

"Through the *commandment*"—holy, righteous, and good, and one's vain efforts to fulfill it—God brings the fallen one to know himself and his condition.

THE LAW BRINGS TO THE HELPLESSNESS OF DEATH

> "Sin . . . working death to me. . . ."
>
> "Sold under sin. . . ."
>
> "In me, that is, in my flesh, dwelleth no good thing."—Verses 13,14,18.

How bitter the strife! How humiliating to the pride of man! "*The law is spiritual*," cries the man, "but I—*I am carnal, sold under sin*." I am practically a slave, for "*what I hate, that I do*" (v. 15).

The very fact that I hate sin proves that my eyes are opened to the beauty and goodness of God's will (v. 16), so that I seem to be like two persons. In my will I desire to do right, but I am utterly *unable* to "do that which is good" (v. 18). Therefore, in one sense, it is not *I* that work the wrong but the sin which reigns and tyrannizes over me (v. 17).

I am truly a slave! What slavery is worse than this? At all events, I know now that "*in me . . . dwelleth no good thing*" (v. 18). I see no man on earth blacker than myself. I can never think again that "I am not as other men." Was ever a soul in such bonds before? The "*good*" I want to do, I do not do; and the "*evil*" which I abhor, I practice (v. 19)!

To sum it all up, I find that "*to me who would do good, evil is present*" (v. 21). I am in the condition that "*I delight* in the law of God after the *inward* man" (v. 22), but I see a different law in my members "*warring against the law of my mind*" (v. 23). I am held as a *slave* under the tyranny of sin.

THE POINT OF DELIVERANCE

> "O wretched man that I am! Who shall deliver me out of this body of death?"—Verse 24, mg.
>
> "I thank God through Jesus Christ our Lord."—Verse 25.

Yes, there is deliverance when the soul is ready to be delivered. The "wretched man" has cried out for help, and in his cry has confessed that he is unable to deliver himself!

The pride of life has been broken down.

The "*inward man*," desiring to obey the law, has not been able to conquer himself or his sins, notwithstanding all his efforts to do "that which is good" in the sight of God. He has failed as yet to apprehend the full message of the cross. He has not seen his death with Christ, and his freedom in Christ from the tyranny of sin and the claims of the law. So in this bitter conflict he has had to find out his need.

Maybe he thought that the "inward man," assisted by the grace of God, would be able to please God—that having begun in the Spirit, by reconciliation with God through the blood of the cross, he could be "perfected" (or grow in grace) by the aid of the flesh!

Not so, you "wretched man." Turn again to Calvary! You need another force within you—the power of the Holy Spirit, and the "law of the Spirit of life in Christ" *alone* can make you free *through the work of Jesus Christ on Calvary.*

The "law" which you have been struggling to obey in your own strength "hath dominion over a man" only for "*so long a time as he liveth*" (Romans 7:1).

You were crucified with your Saviour, you have died with Him, and you are "made *dead* to the law" through the body of Christ.

Yes, "*by faith in the working of God*" (Colossians 2:12). Do you believe this?

Then you are discharged from the claims of the law—"*having died*"! You are "joined to . . . Him who was raised from the dead" (Romans 7:4), and as you rely upon Him to work in you, "the law of the Spirit of life" in Him will make you free (Romans 8:2–3), and "if the Son shall make you free, ye shall be free indeed."

You shall find that "what the law could not do" (Romans 8:3), by commanding you *from without,* God's own Son, sent in your likeness to die in your place, can do *within you*; and the very "requirement of the law" (Romans 8:4, mg.) which you have so utterly failed to obey, shall now be fulfilled in you as you yield to the Spirit of God and "*walk not after the flesh, but after the Spirit.*"

Oh soul, you have lived in ceaseless condemnation. No longer need this be! Those who have cried for deliverance "through Jesus Christ our Lord" and recognized the answer of death within themselves that they should not trust in themselves but in God who raises the dead—for them "there *is* no condemnation." For "*in Christ Jesus*" they experience the force of a new law, an in- working Spirit of life, making them free from the old law with its reign of sin.

"For freedom did Christ set us free: stand fast therefore, and be not entangled again in a yoke of bondage" (Galatians 5:1, mg.). See that you walk step by step in the Spirit, minding "the things of the Spirit" (Romans 8:5). By the power of the Spirit of life which dwells in you, realize the fact that you are a child of the Father, and if a child, then an heir—an heir of God, and joint-heir with Christ, if so be that you suffer with Him, that you may be glorified together (see Romans 8:16–17).

CHAPTER 5

"To this end Christ died and lived again, that He might be Lord."

—Romans 14:9.

CRUCIFIED WITH CHRIST

"I through the law died unto the law, that I might live unto God. I have been crucified with Christ; and it is no longer I that live, but Christ."

—Galatians 2:19–20.

PAUL does not hesitate to refer to his own experience, for he does not preach to the Romans or to the Galatians a gospel *which he has not himself proved.* Now, all that he has written to the Romans concerning the believer's death with Christ he sums up in this personalized passage in his epistle to the Galatians.

To the Romans he said "we" and "our," but to the Galatians he said "I"! "*I* died unto the law," "*I* have been crucified with Christ."

In these words we have embodied the deepest meaning of the deliverance accomplished at Calvary, and the more simply we take the message the more quickly shall we prove the word of the cross as the power of God to deliver.

This "I," which has been the central spring of every human life since the Fall; this "*I,*" cries Paul, was "*crucified with Christ.*" And the law was the means of bringing me to this place of death—the place where I acknowledged my hopeless condition, the place where I ceased from my struggles and cried out for help from another. The "law" brought me to this place where I died to the law by sheer inability to obey it,[2] and from thence I fled to hide myself in the death of Christ . . . and now I have died with Him.

We need to remember that no word of God is exhausted in one application. As we are led on by Him, we find the message of the cross opening out with an ever-widening meaning to meet an ever-deepening need. At first we apprehend our death with Christ simply in relation to the bondage of sin. Initially, with our eyes on the crucified Lord dying for us, we listen to the declaration of Paul in Romans 6:6, "our old man was crucified with Him," and we reckon ourselves dead unto sin and cast away "anger, passion and malice . . . evil-speaking and reviling" (Colossians 3:8, C.H.) and all the manifest "works of the flesh." Thereby we prove with joy that the word of the cross is the power of God to all who believe, and find that the living Christ is "able to save completely them that draw near to God through Him" (Hebrews 7:25, mg.).

But sooner or later we find out that we need a deeper deliverance. Our lives are still in some measure *self*-centered, although we reckon ourselves dead indeed unto sin and find deliverance from the manifest works of the flesh. *Self* shows itself. *Self-energy* or *self-complacency* in service, *self-pity* when we are suffering, *self-seeking* in desiring the praise of men, *self-introspection* and *self-judgment* in hours of trial, *self-sensitiveness* in contact with others, *self-defense* when we are injured. Yes, and sometimes, above all, a *self-consciousness* that makes life almost a burden. These are some of the indignations of the *self*-center within.

In the energy of self, desiring to be wholly the Lord's, we may sometimes consecrate ourselves to Him and with new vigor seek to work for Him oblivious of the *self*-source of our activities, until we are spent out; or, finding little spiritual fruit from all our labor, our eyes are opened to see the uselessness of all our "creaturely activity" for Him (see *Soul and Spirit* and other books).

It is at this point that the Spirit of God brings the "word of the cross" to us with a fresh and blessed message of deliverance—a deliverance that, to some lives, has meant greater consequences than the freedom from the bondage of sin which they proved in earlier days.

The Lord Jesus in His call to the cross touched the *core* of the trouble in every person's life when He said, "If any man would come after Me, let him deny *himself.*" The Lord did not say his *sins*, or certain exterior things. He who knew what was in man struck deeper than actions, to the very center of a man, and said "deny *himself.*"

Let a man renounce *himself* and see *himself* as crucified with Christ, and quickly another Himself—the Lord Christ—will take the central place in the heart and quietly bring all things under His sway!

"Each one of you saith, *I*" (1 Corinthians 1:12), wrote Paul to the Corinthians about the cause of the contentions in that church; and throughout Scripture instance after instance is given of the "I" in its various forms.

"Is not this great Babylon which *I* have built?" (Daniel 4:30), cries Nebuchadnezzar. "*I* will say to my soul . . . take thine ease" (Luke 12:19), says the one whose delight was in earthly treasure. "*I* am not as the rest of men" (Luke 18:11) is the self-estimation of the moral man. "*I am holier* than thou" (Isaiah 65:5), the inner thought of the self-righteous. "*I am rich* . . . and have need of nothing" (Revelation 3:17), the attitude of the self-satisfied. The "*I am*" of this one or that one mirrors the "I" of the Christian who walks "after the manner of men." "For when one saith, *I am of Paul*; and another, *I am of Apollos*; are ye not men?" (see 1 Corinthians 3:1–4) writes the apostle.

But "I" *crucified with Christ* was Paul's charter of freedom. With this message of the cross he met every difficulty of the Christians of his day. "We *who died*," "All *died*," "For *ye died*," was his reiterated statement as he dealt practically with the children of God about their attitude to sin and the elements of the world in the Church of God. And the souls to whom he wrote knew that he lived it out in his *own* life. He did not say "I have been crucified with Christ" and then seek the highest place, even though he might have "claimed honor" (1 Thessalonians 2:6, mg.) as an apostle of Christ.

"I am nothing" he wrote to the Corinthians, and I "am less than the least of all saints," to the Ephesians. *"No longer I"* was the whole spirit of his life, as he counted all things loss for CHRIST and became, as it were, the off-scouring of all things for His dear sake.

For crucified *with Christ* is Paul's invariable declaration, and from whichever point of view he speaks of the results of the death of Christ, he uniformly keeps Calvary as the basal fact. In all his unfolding of truth he never goes beyond the radius of the cross. The Greek word which the apostle uses in Galatians 2:20 (also in Romans 6:6) is a compound form meaning "to crucify *together*," and "crucified *together* with Christ" must be the fact upon which our faith rests if we are to know continuous deliverance. For the eyes of the heart must be focused upon the *crucified Christ* and not be turned inward upon any subjective experience.

"Looking unto Jesus" is the way of deliverance at every stage of the spiritual life. We "look" at the Christ upon His cross, just as the Israelites looked away from their dire condition to the serpent lifted up in the wilderness—look away from ourselves to Calvary for salvation—and as we look we *live.* Again we "look" and see ourselves crucified with Christ, and in the faith which unites us to Him we reckon ourselves dead indeed unto sin and cast away every known sin, refusing to let it reign over us; and—in so far as we honestly *desire* and expect the victory—the Holy Spirit seals our faith with real deliverance.

Once more we look to Calvary and see that we have *died to the law,* for God no longer says "Thou shalt" to those who are in Christ. As we yield obedience to the law of Christ, God sends forth the Spirit of His

Son into our hearts, whereby we cry "Abba Father," and learn to look to Him to supply our every need.

Again we "look" to Calvary, and with clearer vision see *ourselves—"I" crucified with Him*. As the Spirit illuminates the message, we marvel that we did not understand the wondrous secret long before. We have but to make way for the living Christ by taking His cross as *ours* and He will manifest Himself through us.

And is this all? No, no. As He who died and rose again occupies the throne within, in His light we shall see *light*; and as new departments of our complex beings are brought into the searchlight of His Presence, we shall discover ever deeper depths of our need and find Calvary *again and again* the place of life.

"Crucified with Christ!" His cross is mine! I am there with Him. I consent to share His cross, and meet all things with "No longer I!" "I have no longer a separate existence. I am merged in Christ" (Lightfoot), so He, the Living One, will move forth through me, working in me that which is well-pleasing in His sight.

CHAPTER 6

"He shall come to be glorified in His saints, and to be admired in all them that believe."

—2 Thessalonians 1:10, A.V.

THE CROSS AND THE LIVING CHRIST

"I have been crucified with Christ . . . no longer I, but Christ liveth in me."

—Galatians 2:20.

IT was the good pleasure of God to reveal His Son in me," writes the apostle earlier in his epistle to the Galatians. The "mystery which hath been hid from all ages . . . now is manifested to His saints," he writes to the Colossians. It is a mystery which God is *pleased* to make known to His children—"*the riches of the glory of this mystery* . . . which is *Christ in you, the hope of glory*" (Colossians 1:26–27). This is the end, or purpose, of the cross. We are crucified with Christ to *make room* for Him to dwell in our hearts by faith, and this indwelling of the Lord Christ is called a "mystery"—a word signifying "secret," something hid from our understanding until revealed to us.

This mystery was not made known under the Dispensation of Law. Then every man stood by his own "works" before God, except a few like Abraham who in the Spirit foresaw the "day" of Christ and were glad; they saw the promises afar off, and embraced them. But during the Dispensation of the Church it is God's purpose that the "mystery" should be proclaimed to all nations, that those who are "obedient to the faith" (see Romans 16:25–26) may share its glory.

Paul said he was made a minister to "fulfill the word [or purpose] of God, even the mystery"; and his burden of heart was that others should "gain in all its richness the full assurance of understanding; truly to know the mystery of God" (Colossians 2:2, C.H.) which "*by revelation was made known*" (Ephesians 3:3, C.H.) to him. Especially the eternal purpose of God, that men of *every* tongue and tribe and nation were to share in the unsearchable riches of Christ. Paul said it was a special gift of grace to him that he should be chosen by God to bear among all nations such glad tidings, and to bring "light to all," that each might behold the "*stewardship of the mystery*"—the trust given to each to whom it is revealed to carry the message to all people, "to the intent that to the principalities and powers" in the heavenly realm (who are watching the dealings of God with a fallen creation) may be made known "through the Church" the manifold wisdom of God (Ephesians 3:10).

The revelation of Christ in Paul was given that he might "preach *Him*," he declares to the Galatians, and he precedes his testimony, "Christ *liveth* in me," by the words "*I have been crucified with Christ*," showing clearly that the revelation of the mystery of Christ living in us depends upon a true and real planting into His death.

Once the believer perceives this focal point of Calvary in relation to his practical experience, all the truths of God fall into their place in beautiful harmony.

No ideal of life is too high, since the believer has but to make way for the Lord Himself to *fulfill the ideal through him*. No command of God for service is too great, since the Christ Himself becomes all wisdom and power within him, as he by faith retires, so to speak, to the cross, and then moves forward to each service in reliance upon the indwelling Lord. The very *energy* of God comes into his life, and as he proves with joy the might of the risen Christ thus working through him, his whole outlook changes. "*I have been taught the secret . . . I can do all things in Him*" (Philippians 4:12–13, C.H.), becomes the glad triumphant cry; "To me *life is Christ*" (Philippians 1:21, C.H.), the one increasing joy; "I will speak only of the works which *Christ has wrought by me*" (Romans 15:18, C.H.), the simple testimony; "I labor in earnest conflict according to *His working* which works in me with mighty power" (Colossians 1:29, C.H.), the energizing spirit of service day by day.

Oh blessed life! How restful, how glad, how free, when once the secret is known, and the soul learns to live by faith in the Son of God.

But, Paul, does this mean that you have become a machine with no personal choice or desires?

"Crucified . . . *yet I live*," cries Paul. I am not a mummy, nor a machine! I am a human being with feelings and personal wishes, hopes and desires.

I live all the *more* because I have died; for the sensibilities of this human organism, dulled by slavery to sin, have now become freed to become acute and living. *Freed* is my condition—not to be any longer the medium of self-sensitiveness, self-seeking or self-love but the quickened vehicle for the manifestation of the love and life of the Christ who now "*liveth in me*."

"*Me*"—Paul the apostle—who am not worthy to be called an apostle, for I persecuted the Church of God.

"*Me*," with all my own characteristics, temperament and tastes. All that goes to make up the personality of "*me*." Christ lives in *me*.

Nevertheless I know it is no longer "I" that is the moving spring and center of my life. It is "*not I*," but the grace of God which enables me to labor more abundantly than all the other apostles. It is not *my* life but the life which flows from the living *Christ,* who dwells within my heart, that is manifested through me.

But Paul, is this a wonderful consciousness to you? Do you *feel* "dead," and do you realize great joy and heavenly ecstasy through the risen Lord thus dwelling in your heart?

No, "that life which I now live in the flesh [body] I live in *faith.*"

But what kind of faith, Paul? Is it by *your* faith that you have experienced death with Christ, and is this faith a great effort or strain every moment?

No, it is "*the faith which is in the Son of God, who loved me, and gave Himself up for me.*"

Ah, blessed proof of "I" being crucified with Christ! The "I" passes from the horizon of the soul's vision, and the Son of God, in the great love shown by His death on the cross, fills the whole heart and mind.

"*He gave Himself up for me*" becomes the dominating thought of one's life, and all things are seen in the light and love of

Calvary. Abandonment to the pierced hands of Him who died brings nothing but the sweetest joy; and, occupied with the *object* of love, one's faith in Him becomes a spontaneous, unconscious attitude of the soul. The believer no longer is concerned with his *own* experience or cares for anything on earth *purely in relation to himself*, but longs with deep desire that *He who died* should see the fruit resulting from *His* travail on Calvary's cross and be satisfied.

THE WAY OF FAITH

> "I live in the faith of the Son of God."—Galatians 2:20, C.H.

> "Before whose eyes Jesus crucified was openly set forth. . . . Received ye the Spirit . . . by works . . . or by . . . faith?"—Galatians 3:1–2, mg.

Paul says that the "outward life which still remains" (Galatians 2:20, C.H.) he lives "in *the faith of the Son of God*." Even his own *act* of faith seems to have passed out of the range of his consciousness, by the assured knowledge of Christ living and working in him. The risen Lord, taking possession of the believer, brings with Him the "*spirit of faith*," and the act of moment-by-moment trust should eventually become as spontaneous and simple as breathing.

But there are *transition* stages in the spiritual life—when the soul is being led into deeper knowledge of itself and its own powerlessness that it may know the abounding resources in the risen Lord. In such times of transition the believer has often to cling in an extremity of trial to the bare word of God that he is crucified with Christ. Fresh transactions with God will ofttimes be necessary, when he commits himself *anew* to Him and trusts Him to fulfill in him His highest purposes—times when he, so to speak, casts upon the Faithful God the *responsibility* of bringing him out through all the testings into the larger places of the life in Christ.

We must, at all times, take heed in our dealings with God that our faith is always in the *present tense*. By this we mean that as we lay hold of His word that we *were* carried to the cross with the Crucified One, we should definitely believe that He "who quickeneth the dead, and calleth the things that *are not* as though they *were*" (Romans 4:17) does by His own creative word *now* communicate and maintain the life of Christ in us. With Jehovah, *speaking is doing*. He said at the creation of the world, "Let there be," and there was. The word of the cross from the mouth of God is as much the word of omnipotence as the word spoken at creation. Jehovah points to His Son upon the cross and speaks the word "*crucified with Him*"; the soul responds with "Amen, so be it." And by this the message of the cross becomes the power of God in all who thus believe.

In times of transition also the believer is apt to turn from the *way of faith* to "works of law"—or self-effort. The turning back to "works of law" was the danger of the Galatian Christians. Possibly the first joyous experience of the Holy Spirit's work in them had passed away, and not understanding clearly the full purpose of Christ's death and the way of faith in the crucified and risen Lord, they were in a condition to fall an easy prey to those who sought to draw them back to the old life of reliance upon self and its doings.

The apostle's appeal to them shows clearly that the turning away of their vision from Calvary was the cause of their peril, and through his words we see also that the work of Christ on the cross must be the anchor of the soul along the whole course of the Christian life.

"I placarded Christ crucified before your eyes!" (Lightfoot). "O foolish Galatians, who has bewitched you?" (Galatians 3:1), exclaims the apostle, as he thinks of the way in which Jesus Christ was "openly set forth crucified" among them, for he surely had not proclaimed to them less than the full gospel he had preached to the Corinthians and the Romans. How they could forget such an unveiling of Christ's death and turn back upon themselves, he did not know.

Who drew your eyes away from Calvary and all that it means? Who *"fascinated you?"* (Galatians 3:1, C.H.). Some subtle influence has come upon you. *"Are you so foolish?"* the apostle cries. With their vision turned toward Him who died, they had received the Spirit by simply believing the "message of faith" (Galatians 3:2, mg.), and they had *proved* the "word of the cross" to be the energy of

God, for God had supplied the Spirit bountifully to them, and even worked "*miracles in*" (Galatians 3:5, mg.) them, in response to their "hearing of faith" (Galatians 3:5).

As Jesus Christ had thus been "painted large upon His cross to their very eyes," had they not learned the meaning of His death? Before the way of faith was revealed, they were "*shut up in prison . . . under the law*" (Galatians 3:23, C.H.) because they could not fulfill the law; but on the cross Christ redeemed them and became accursed for their sakes, so that in response to *faith alone* they might receive the Holy Spirit (Galatians 3:13–14) to work in them continually. Did they not know that they became children of God "through *faith* in Christ Jesus," and as many as had been "*baptized into Christ*" did "put on" Christ, that is, had "clothed" themselves with Christ? (Galatians 3:27, C.H.)?

Were all their past sufferings in vain? Were they going back to be prison-bound souls under the whip of the law instead of entering in to all the privileges of sons of God? "*I am again bearing the pangs of travail for you, till Christ be fully formed within you*" (Galatians

4:19, C.H.), Paul cries in the anguish of his soul. "How senseless to go back from the simplicity of reliance upon Christ to reliance upon self and its doings. I can only attribute this to some evil power which has ensnared you, some specious influence which has drawn you away from Calvary."

Alas, such a subtle influence is at work today among the people of God, turning away *their* vision from Christ crucified!

The adversary of souls knows how to "fascinate" and, insensibly to ourselves, to draw us away from the cross of Calvary. His devices are innumberable, and every stage of growth in the spiritual life is attacked by him with this particular snare; for every distortion of truth and working of error may be traced to the failure to keep Calvary, and its twofold message, as the *central fact of the believer's life.*

This is the *central truth* from which every other aspect of the truth of God radiates. All other "lines of truth" must be allowed never to be carried to their extreme limit but kept within the radius of the *cross.*

A continuous looking off to Jesus Christ *crucified,* and a steadfast dependence upon the Spirit of God to work in us the separating power of His death and to minister to us the quickening of His life, is the "way of faith" in which Christ can be "fully formed within" and the believer grow up unto the "measure of the stature of the fullness of Christ."

O soul, redeemed by the precious blood of Christ, if the "word of the cross" has come to you in the power of God, and you have consented to be crucified together with the Crucified One and truly united to Him as the risen Lord, take heed that you are. Day by day, turn your heart's vision toward the cross, praising the Triune God that you are there with the One who died, and then—

1) ***By faith in the working of God, commit to the death of the cross,*** without delay, any aspect of the old life revealed to you, counting upon the Holy Spirit to bear witness to the death of Christ by saving you from the accursed thing. Always respond promptly to anything that is shown to you as being not of God, during the whole course of your spiritual life, for His light will then shine upon your ways and you will see even your "comeliness" to be corruption as you walk in the light of God.

2) ***By faith in the faithfulness of God live in the present moment alone,*** and, counting upon the Holy Spirit to communicate to you the life of Jesus, cast yourself upon His strength, and do the "next thing" that lies in your path of duty—believing that it is God who works in you to will and to do according to His good pleasure. If you do miss step with your Lord, trust Him, by the skillfulness of His hands, to put you in step again, and do not whip yourself with vain regrets but continue in His love and leave yourself entirely in His keeping.

3) ***By faith in the risen Christ walk on with Him,*** refusing all temptation to look within or turn back upon yourself at all. Let His word dwell in you richly, teaching you His will for your manner of life, and pour out your heart's longings to Him that He might show Himself through you to all around.

4) ***By faith you stand. Be not high-minded, but fear.*** No past experience of His grace will avail you should you turn from simple dependence upon your Lord. You have no power but what you receive from Him hour by hour. You have a watchful foe, ready to ensnare you if you but give him place. Keep yourself safely hidden in your Lord who intercedes for you before the throne of God; for if you will walk in the light, bringing to the light your doings—that it may be shown to you whether they are "*wrought in God*" (John 3:21)—the blood of Jesus Christ His Son will keep cleansing you from all sin, and you shall walk in blessed fellowship with Him.

> "Let us hold fast the confession of our hope that it waver not, for He is faithful that promised" (Hebrews 10:23). "If we are faithless, He abideth faithful; for He cannot deny Himself" (2 Timothy 2:13).

CHAPTER 7

"He showed unto them His hands and His side. . . . He breathed on them, and saith unto them, Receive ye the Holy Spirit."

—John 20:20–22.

THE CROSS AND THE HOLY SPIRIT

"Christ redeemed us from the curse . . . having become a curse for us . . . that we might receive the promise of the Spirit."

—Galatians 3:13–14.

THESE words of the apostle Paul, in his letter to the Galatians, show that the gift of the Holy Spirit is based upon the work of Christ on the cross of Calvary.

The Spirit of truth, who proceeds from the Father (John 15:26), is sent by the Son to each of His redeemed ones for the special purpose of *teaching them* the things of God (John 14:26), for *reminding them* of the words of Christ, for always and only *bearing witness* to Christ (John 14:26), and for *guiding* each soul into all the truth. He speaks not of Himself, but communicates the mind of the Father and the Son to those of whom He has charge (John 16:13–14), unveiling to them the eternal purposes of God. He glorifies Christ in all His redeemed, taking of all His fullness and declaring it unto them.

It was in the upper room in Jerusalem, on His resurrection day, that Jesus Himself came and stood in the midst of His disciples. Showing them His hands and His side with the marks of His cross upon them, "He breathed on them, and saith unto them, *Receive ye the Holy Spirit*" (John 20:19–22). Again after the Ascension, being "by the right hand of God exalted," He received from the Father the promise of the Holy Spirit and poured Him forth upon that waiting group on earth who had "*with one accord*" continued steadfastly in prayer, waiting for the "*promise of the Father*" which the Lord had said would come to them to equip them for the work, in cooperation with the Spirit, of witnessing to the death and resurrection of the Son of God.

How the Spirit of God taught the disciples and illuminated to them the words of Christ; how He guided them into truth wholly foreign to their preconceived ideas and environment; how He bore witness to the Christ, and communicated the mind and will of Father and Son to the redeemed on earth; how He glorified the Christ and took of His fullness and declared it unto them—the book of the Acts of the Apostles sets forth.

Through the apostle Paul, faithfully taught by the Spirit, we learn that His dwelling in and possessing every believing soul is on the ground of Calvary alone. "*Christ redeemed us*," he writes, "*that we might receive the . . . Spirit*." The word "redeemed" takes us back to Calvary, where we were redeemed "with precious blood, as of a lamb without blemish and without spot, even the blood of Christ" (1 Peter 1:19). Not only so, but the Christ became a *curse* for us, that we might receive the Spirit! He redeemed us "having become accursed for our sakes (for it is written, 'Cursed is every one that hangeth on a tree') *to the end* . . . that through faith we might receive the promise of the Spirit" (Galatians 3:13–14, C.H.).

The twofold message of Calvary is thus clearly linked with the gift of the Holy Spirit, for if Christ became a curse for us, then *we are the accursed ones* on whose behalf He hung upon a tree; and as our Representative, He carried us to the tree with Him.

That the curse of the cross is associated with the promise of the Spirit is also deeply suggestive of the conditions upon which He can freely work in us. For it is only when we realize in very truth that we are "accursed" in all that we are in ourselves that we gladly accept the message of Calvary that we are crucified with Him who died on our behalf and make room for the full indwelling and outworking of the Holy Spirit.

"*The cross leads to the Spirit, and the Spirit back again to the cross*" (Andrew Murray). Only through the death of Christ can the soul receive the Spirit; and only by the Holy Spirit, thus received, can the believer be vitally united with the death of Christ so as to know with assurance the indwelling of the risen Lord and be able to say with truth, "I have been crucified with Christ—Christ liveth in me!" Yet again it is true that *only through a still deeper fellowship* with Christ in His cross can we know the Holy Spirit in fullness and power.

Paul's words to the Galatians illustrate this also, for he appeals to his preaching about Calvary as the ground of the Holy Spirit's work in them. And yet it is evident that although they had manifestly received the Spirit, they needed a *clearer* knowledge of the cross, for if they had seen their death with Christ as fully as Paul had done, they would not have been disposed to return to the old plane of self-effort. The Galatians had not realized the *curse* of the law which came upon every soul who failed even in one point of obedience to the law, and so they had not come to an end of all self-reliance. They had *begun* "in the Spirit" but did not know how to *live* "in the Spirit" on that very same ground of faith in the crucified Son of God which had brought Him into their lives at the beginning.

It is urgent that Paul's words to the Galatian believers come with renewed emphasis today, for many of the children of God need a clearer vision of the cross of Calvary in relation to the Holy Spirit's working within the soul. For the Holy Spirit *works upon the basis of Calvary alone,* and the extent of the apprehension of all that the death of Christ means for those whom He redeemed is the extent of His possession of the individual believer.

The cross leads to the Spirit! Through the atoning work of Christ, every yielded heart may receive the Holy Spirit; and in response to the *surrender* of the recipient does He take possession, "cleansing [the] heart by faith" (Acts 15:9).

The Spirit leads to the cross! This is clearly outlined in the life of the Lord Christ. The heavens were opened and the Holy Spirit came upon Jesus at His baptism in Jordan, when (as a type) He entered the waters of death and chose to be identified with sinners; but this was not the real Calvary. It was "*through the Eternal Spirit*" who came upon Him at Jordan that Jesus also steadfastly set His face to go to Jerusalem and was enabled to drink the actual cup of death at Calvary. After the cross, by the Spirit of God He was quickened and raised from the dead, thus to receive at the right hand of the

Father the anointing above His fellows. This is also the pattern for all who will follow in His steps. Through our surrender to God and the acceptance of the cross—typified by Jordan—the Holy Spirit gains possession of the citadel of the heart; and then He seeks to lead the believer into the real fellowship of the cross, working in steady progression from within to without, from center to circumference—dealing with new departments of the life, unveiling new needs and revealing the cross in aspect after aspect as the answer to those needs. He applies the death of Christ as the severing power from the old life and ministers the life of the risen Christ for the building up of the new creation.

The believer may be said to be "*filled*" with the Spirit when he first receives the Spirit, but he is filled only to the extent of his capacity at the time. The capacity may be small, and it will *remain small* unless he apprehends that the Spirit leads to the cross, so that the capacity may be deepened and a greater fullness of the Holy Spirit be truly known.

From faith to faith the Holy Spirit leads the trusting one as he cooperates with Him by a glad and ready "yes" to all His dealings, until, at the appearing of the Lord from heaven, the body of humiliation itself is transformed and made like unto His glorious body; or should physical death be the will of God for the redeemed one, the Holy Spirit ministers such abundant life in Christ that he does not "see death" but only falls asleep, to be "forever with the Lord." Mortality is then "*swallowed up of life*." "Now he that *wrought us for this very thing* is God, who gave unto us the earnest of the Spirit" (2 Corinthians 5:4–5).

FILLED UNTO THE FULLNESS OF GOD

> "He would grant you strength by the entrance of His Spirit into your inner man, that Christ may dwell in your hearts by faith . . . and to know the love of Christ . . . that you may be filled therewith, even to the measure of the fullness of God."—Ephesians 3:16–19, C.H.

These words sum up in brief the purpose of the work of the Holy Spirit in the believer. Paul prays for the Ephesians that they may be "*strengthened with power*" through the Spirit, "that Christ may dwell" in their hearts by faith. The Eternal Spirit of the Father takes possession of the redeemed one for the express purpose of revealing the indwelling of the Son. He *strengthens* the believer for the fulfillment of the conditions necessary for the Christ to be fully formed within—the conditions we have already seen as explained in Paul's words to the Galatians, "I have been crucified with Christ—Christ liveth in me."

Faith on the part of the redeemed one is again mentioned here. Faith is nonexistent apart from its object. Faith is simply reliance upon the word of God, with the character of God at the back of His word! "Faith cometh by *hearing*," and is awakened in the receptive heart by the Spirit of God Himself as He speaks the word of God to the soul. "*You were made partakers of His resurrection, through the faith wrought in you by God,* who raised Him" (Colossians 2:12, C.H.), wrote Paul to the Colossians.

We are therefore cast upon the Holy Spirit to supply to us all our need, including even the very faith by which we are to cooperate with Him and appropriate all that the Lord Christ has accomplished for us in His death on the cross.

Unbelief is described by the Lord as sin, though we more often bewail it is as an "infirmity" which must be borne as an affliction by the poor soul under its power. But we must deal with unbelief as *sin*; confess it to God as *sin*; renounce it as *sin*; and expect deliverance from it through the death of Christ as much as from *any* acknowledged sin.

Let us look once more to Calvary. We are *crucified* with Christ, therefore let us count upon Him as the living One to give us the "*spirit of faith*." And then, ceasing from our own works in struggling to "believe," let us rest—lie down, so to speak—upon His word, and we shall be given a childlike, trustful confidence in Him and be taught to live in the faith of the Son of God, even as He lived by the Father.

As Christ is thus revealed within the soul the Spirit of God leads the believer on, and he is made "*strong to apprehend*" with all saints the breadth, length, height and depth of the love of Christ. The supreme manifestation of that love was blazoned forth in His death on Calvary. "*Strong* to apprehend!" Divine strength is needed, for the apprehending comes only by the sharing of His sufferings. The apprehending of another's sorrows with the mind alone does not create the fellowship that is engendered by walking the same path. "*Ye shall indeed drink of My cup*," said the Master to His disciples.

But to be "strong to *apprehend*" something of the love that led Christ to Calvary is not all. "That ye may be *filled therewith*," writes the apostle. And to what extent, Paul? "*Even to the measure of the fullness of God!*"

But this is beyond our power to grasp, O faithful apostle of the cross. Yes, but "He is able to do exceeding abundantly above all that we ask," or even "think"—for the mere conceptions of the mind have no place here! "According to the power that worketh in us" (Ephesians 3:20). We can be filled with the love of Christ—filled, and filled, and filled unto all the Fullness of God, yea, as when "the waters were risen, waters to swim in!" (Ezekiel 47:5).

"Oh that I knew this blessed life!" may be the cry in the heart of some who read these words. Child of God, if you are vainly trying to realize the deliverance of Calvary without reliance upon the inworking Spirit of God, open your whole being to Him and commit yourself into His hands. Yield to Him to vitally unite you to the Crucified One, and to reveal within you the living Lord.

Are you willing for implicit obedience to Him at any cost? Will you let Him have full right of way in your life? Are you now ready for the *message of faith*? Then once more turn to Calvary. As you look away to Him who died, dare to believe the written word of God that you *have* died with Him and God's wisdom in a mystery will be un-veiled to you by the Eternal Spirit.

"But what is the *anointing* of the Spirit?"

Are you in the service of the King? As the Holy Spirit reveals the Christ in you, you shall understand that your Lord not only dwells in you but that you are a member of the Body of Christ; and as you are brought into your place in the Body, the holy oil which anointed the Christ above His fellows will flow down to the skirts of His garments, even upon and through you, anointing you for all service in the will of God. The Christ Himself will work through you mightily by the Holy Spirit as you abandon yourself to His will. But remember: "There are *diversities of gifts,* but the same Spirit"; "*diversities of workings,* but the same God, who worketh all things in all." "All [are the work of] . . . the same Spirit, dividing to each one severally even as He will" (see 1 Corinthians 12:4–11).

The Son of God was anointed with the oil of gladness above His fellows because He "loved righteousness and hated iniquity" (Hebrews 1:9). Even so will the Christ bring you into a deep hatred of sin and a love of all that pertains to the righteousness of God; you will love your Lord not only as a God of love but also as the God of terrible holiness. You will covet the severity of God upon all in yourself that is unlike Him and gladly be chastened that you may become a partaker of His holiness. So shall you become united in closer bonds to your Lord and a sharer in the anointing of Him whose scepter is a scepter of "rightness" or "straitness" (Hebrews 1:8, A.V., mg.).

Knowing that you have given room to the Holy Spirit, now walk step by step in the Spirit, depending alone upon Him and seeking only His will and pleasure; so will He lead you on and teach you how to abide in your Lord, being adjusted into *your* place in His mystical Body. And you shall know that "the anointing which *ye have received of Him* abideth in you . . . the [very] anointing [which] teacheth you of all things, and is truth, and is no lie; and even as it hath taught you, ye shall abide in Him" (1 John 2:27, A.V.).

CHAPTER 8

"Present yourselves UNTO GOD, *as alive from the dead, and your members as weapons . . .* UNTO GOD."

—Romans 6:13, mg.

THE LIFE SIDE OF THE CROSS

"One died for all, therefore all died; and He died for all that they which live should no longer live unto themselves, but unto Him."

—2 Corinthians 5:14–15.

IT has been well said that there are two sides to the cross: the earthward side, which means the negative deliverance by *death,* and the heavenward side, which tells of *life* in union with the living Lord. As the substitution of Christ *for* sin and the death with Christ *to* sin are, for all who believe in Him, *indivisible,* so death and life are not to be divided along the whole course of the Christian life.

"If we have become *united with Him by the likeness of His death*," writes Paul to the Romans, "we shall be also with Him *in resurrection*." It is, as we have seen, the work of the Holy Spirit to make us really "*partakers of a vital union*" sharing "*the reality of His death*"—as real a union "as that of a graft with the tree into which it is grafted" (Romans 6:5, Conybeare note).

What such a vital union means can only be known by the working of the Holy Spirit in response to a faith which rests upon the work of Christ on the cross of Calvary.

The Holy Spirit will wield the "word of the cross," which is "*living, and active, and sharper than any two-edged sword*," and with it pierce even to the dividing of soul and spirit, of both joints and marrow, revealing the thoughts and intents of the heart—separating the old from the new life, until the life which is from above has unhindered sway and the redeemed one truly lives on the life side of the cross.

But we must remember that there is no "resurrection life" apart from the risen Lord. We are planted into "*His death*"; it is *with*

Him that we were crucified, and *to Him* as the Living One we are joined so that *in Him* as our sphere we may walk in newness of life. The resurrection life is also a continuous one. It is not an experience which we passed through at some crisis long ago, but union with a living Christ—*Himself* the Resurrection—abiding in us and putting forth His mighty energy through us, so far as we fulfill the conditions which permit Him to do so.

Moreover, life cannot be *copied*, and no assertion of possessing resurrection life can bring it into being. But no assertion of life is *needed* when it is present, for it is its own witness by its manifesting power.

Thanks be to God, the life in union with Christ is *real life*, a dynamic power that is indisputable, bringing the soul into such living relationship with the risen Christ as to make it know something of the "*powers of the age to come*," and so to see the things of time from the standpoint of eternity as to lift it above the attractions and absorbing interests of things on the earth.

On the resurrection side of the cross, the Holy Spirit illumines the cross of Calvary until "Jesus Christ crucified" becomes "placarded" before the eyes of the heart, and the soul is ever being taught fresh aspects of His death; for until deliverance from the bondage of sin is known, with the consequent cleansing of heart and life, the Lord is not given His place on the throne in the heart and the deeper lessons of Calvary cannot be imparted by the Holy Spirit. In 2 Corinthians 5:14 and subsequent verses, the apostle Paul gives a word picture of the life on the resurrection side of the cross and clearly sets forth the death on Calvary as the basis for this new life from God.

THE MOTIVE POWER OF THE NEW LIFE

> "The love of Christ constraineth us."—Verse 14.

The word "constraineth," which Paul uses, occurs several times in New Testament Greek to express a "grip" or constraint which is overpowering or irresistible. It is rendered "strait" in Philippians 1:23, and is the word used by the Lord Himself when He speaks of the baptism of suffering before Him and says He is "straitened" until it is accomplished (Luke 12:50).

It is the word used in describing the grip of the "men that *held* Jesus" (Luke 22:63), and used again of the people "*holden*" with great fear at the presence of Christ and of Simon's wife's mother "*holden*" with a great fever.

These instances, and their connection, give light upon the sense in which the word is used by Paul when speaking of the love of Christ constraining him. It keeps him in a "strait," hemmed in to one course from which there is no deviation. He is "held" by this great love; completely *mastered* by it, so that he is urged and impelled onward into one course like a torrent sweeping down everything that comes in its way.

Such was certainly the love of Christ, for He who was on an equality with God counted it not a prize to be grasped but emptied Himself and humbled Himself to become, in the likeness of man, obedient unto death—even the death of the cross.

And this love is the *motive power* of the new life in union with the living Lord: a love shed abroad in the heart by the Holy Spirit, a love which casts aside all self-love and self-interest and completely holds the soul in its power.

THE BASIS OF THE NEW LIFE

> "One died for all, therefore ALL died."—Verse 14.

As is his custom, Paul clearly shows the death of Christ to be the *basis* of the new life. In no other passage does he condense the twofold message of the cross into such a terse sentence. The Saviour was the substitute for sinners—*He "died for all"*; and all for whom He died, died with Him—*"therefore all died."*

"The love of Christ constrains me," cries Paul, because I have been to Calvary, and in the death of the Man who died I have seen my death too. I have died *with* Him, and in fellowship with Him in His death all selfish barriers have been broken away. The love that led Jesus to Calvary is the love which has been shed abroad in my heart by the Holy Spirit, and now it constrains me as it constrained *Him* and pressed *Him* onward to the cross.

THE OBJECT OF THE NEW LIFE

> "He died for all, that they which live should no longer live unto themselves, but unto Him who for their sakes died and rose again."—2 Corinthians 5:15.

They who have "died" with Him now "*live*" in His life. They realize that it was "for *their sakes*" He died, "for *their sakes*" He lives; so for *His sake* they gladly consent no longer to live unto themselves but unto Him.

They see that they have been crucified with Him, and now He who died and rose again fills their whole vision, constraining them to present their bodies as a living sacrifice, "holy, acceptable unto God," which is their glad and "reasonable sacrifice."

THE SEVERING POWER OF THE CROSS

> "Wherefore we henceforth know no man after the flesh."—Verse 16.

In the light of the cross, Paul looks out at the world of men from a different standpoint to that which he held when as a Pharisee he walked in the streets of Jerusalem.

Then he was a "Hebrew of Hebrews." He would have "no dealing with Samaritans." But all his exclusive caste-prejudice has passed away in the light of Calvary and because of his life in union with the risen Lord. "Henceforth I know no man after the flesh," cries Paul—for I live now in the sphere where all distinctions are done away, where there "can be neither Jew nor Greek . . . but all are one in Christ Jesus."

Paul is separated still from men, in truth, but not now with the exclusive holiness which said "Stand by thyself, I am holier than thou." Rather, he is separated unto God by the indwelling Presence of the Holy One Himself. Yet living unto God he is *nearer to men*, for he sees them as souls "for whom Christ died," and knows that there is "*no distinction* between Jew and Greek" in His sight, for "*the same Lord is Lord of all*," and is "*rich unto all that call upon Him*." He is separated by the cross from earth-born exclusive pride to be toward all men *in Christ's stead*, and, as was his Lord, the servant of all.

Paul recognizes, however, the possibility of a knowledge of Christ "after the flesh," a state from which the cross severs by the power of the Holy Spirit. This knowledge of Christ is, so to speak, an *exterior* knowledge, even as the disciples knew Him before Calvary—knowing Him and yet not knowing Him as He *really* was within the veil of His human body.

Even so today is it possible to know the historical Christ. His life, His death, His resurrection and ascension, all may be exterior facts, known to the mind but exercising no real power in the life. Participation with Christ's death changes all this, for on the *life side* of the cross the Holy Spirit reveals the *risen* Lord, and He is known "after the Spirit" as the *Living* One.

THE NEW LIFE IN CHRIST

> "Wherefore if any man is IN CHRIST, there is a new creation: the old things are passed away; behold, they are become new."—Verse 17, mg.

The "wherefore" in verses 16 and 17 both point back to verse 14. If any man is in Christ—baptized *into His death*—through the gateway of the cross he thus enters the sphere where Christ becomes his *environment* as well as his new source of life. Joined to the living Christ, for him old things pass away, for *in Christ* there is a *new* creation, not just a mending or improving of the old.

On the *life side* of the cross the soul united to the living Christ is said to put on the "*new man*" (Colossians 3:10–11).

By the *daily supply of the Spirit of Jesus* (Philippians 1:19) the "new man" "grows continually to a more perfect knowledge and likeness of his Creator" (Colossians 3:10–11, C.H.) and grows up "*after the image of Him that created him*," in the sphere where "Christ is all and in all." A child naturally grows up in the likeness of his father, and the new life communicated to the redeemed grows up in the likeness of Him who is the Creator of the new creation—*if*, that is, the death with Christ is inflinchingly recognized and "old things" are truly allowed to pass away to make room for the growth of the new man "which is after God . . . created in righteousness, and holiness of truth" (Ephesians 4:24, mg.).

THE NEW SERVICE FOR OTHERS

> "All things are of God who . . . *placed* in us the word of reconciliation. We are ambassadors therefore on behalf of Christ."—Verses 18–20, mg.

It is to the *new man* in Christ—who clearly knows his separation unto God and meets no man any longer on earthly ground but in the name of Him who died for all—that God commits "*the ministry of reconciliation*." The alternative reading in the A.S.V. margin is suggestive, for it says that God places *in* His ambassadors the message of the cross—the "word of reconciliation."

It is written upon their hearts, wrought into their very beings, even as Ezekiel "ate the roll" before he spoke forth the very words of God to Israel. Even so are Christ's ambassadors prepared that they may truly speak on behalf of Christ "in God's stead."

Through them the "word of the cross" is manifestly the power of God, for they are "*working together with Him*" who through them entreats the souls for whom He died that they not "receive the grace of God in vain" but give heed to His call in this day of salvation.

THE OUTWARD LIFE DEPICTED

> "Giving no occasion of stumbling . . . but in everything commending ourselves."—2 Corinthians 6:3–4.

As we have moved on from the basis of the new life, given in 5:14, we have seen depicted, in steady progression, the characteristics of this life which springs from Calvary and is lived in union with Him who died and rose again.

"*No longer unto self*" is the fixed decision; "*unto Him who for my sake died*," the unvarying aim; "*I see all souls as those for whom He died,*" the principle of action toward others; "*old things have passed away,*" the continual attitude to the past; "*He has placed in me the word of reconciliation,*" the constant responsibility to others; "*I must work together with Him,*" the restraining and watching attitude day by day.

"*No longer unto self*" is shown in vivid object lesson in the brief sketch of the apostle's own life which follows (see 2 Corinthians 6:4–10). His outward circumstances meant afflictions, hardships, distresses, stripes, imprisonments, tumults, labors, watchings, fastings; but the new life was manifested in much patience, pureness, knowledge of God, longsuffering and kindness—a life truly lived "in the Holy Spirit," in genuine love, speaking the word of truth in the manifested power of God.

Protected by the armor of righteousness on every side, Paul had lived this life through glory and dishonor, through evil report and good report. He had been counted as a deceiver, and yet he was true; he was unknown, and yet well known; as dying, and yet, behold, he lived by the daily-renewed power of the life within him. He was chastened with keenest suffering, yet not killed—for the enemy could not touch his life. He was sorrowful over all the need of the dying world, yet was always rejoicing in Him whom he had learned to know. He was poor in every way, but making many rich with eternal treasure; having nothing in or for himself, yet possessing all things in Christ, in whom are hid *all* the treasures of wisdom and knowledge.

There is no room for *living unto self* in this pattern, O child of God. And so far as you are truly united to your Lord and made conformable to His death, you shall know in your measure this life which springs from Calvary—and walk even as Jesus walked, to the glory and praise of God.

Measure thy life by loss instead of gain;

Not by the wine drunk, but the wine poured forth;

For love's strength standeth in love's sacrifice—

And whoso suffers most hath most to give.

CHAPTER 9

"Jesus . . . suffered without the gate. Let us therefore go forth unto Him without the camp, bearing His reproach."

—Hebrews 13:12–13.

CRUCIFIED TO THE WORLD

"Far be it from me to glory, save in the cross of our Lord Jesus Christ, through which [whom, mg.] the world hath been crucified unto me, and I unto the world."

—Galatians 6:14.

ON the resurrection side of Calvary, the apostle looks out upon the world and sees the cross once more in its separating power standing between him and the world. Viewing the light of God streaming down upon Calvary, he cries, "God forbid that I should glory, save in the cross." The apostle is driven to this outburst by the memory of some who were shirking persecution associated with the cross. The cross was an "offense" in a special way in the days of Paul, for it offered salvation full and free to all men, Jew or Gentile, apart from the external rite of circumcision. This meant the end of Judaism with its exclusiveness and its carnal commandments. The One who is in essence Spirit henceforth sought worshipers to worship Him in spirit and in truth, disciples who would offer Him spiritual sacrifices of praise in the spiritual temple of the heart (John 4:23–24).

To preach such a gospel of necessity means offense, and the pleasing of Christ rather than men.

No, more. "*I have been crucified* with Christ even to the *religious* world," cries Paul. "If I preach the cross as the Lord Christ has unveiled it to me, I see that His cross will be the instrument of my crucifixion as it was of His. In truth, I have already suffered the loss of all things, but God forbid that I should think at all of my sufferings for Christ; rather, let me glory in His sufferings for me. In the light of all that Calvary meant to *Him,* the offense of the cross is my proudest boast."

Lightfoot puts it this way: "God forbid that I should glory in anything save in the cross of Christ. On that cross I have been crucified to the world, and the world had been crucified to me. Henceforth we are dead each to the other. In Christ Jesus, old things have passed away. Circumcision is nothing, and uncircumcision is nothing. All external distinctions have vanished. The new spiritual creation is all in all."

Such a view of Calvary as this is only to be known on the *life* side of the cross, when in the light of God it stands out in all its glory as the wisdom and power of God.

In early days we shrink from the demands of the cross, for it only seems to speak of separation and death; but as the soul walks in intimate fellowship with the Living One, His death on Calvary becomes illuminated with heavenly light, and the vision grows more and more acute to see into the depths of the sufferings of Christ and the glories that shall follow, "which things angels desire to look into" (1 Peter 1:12).

To Paul the cross is, as it were, a great gulf fixed between him and every phase of "this present evil world." Crucified with Christ, he is not only delivered from the tyranny of sin and the claims of the law, but from the *world itself* in all its aspects.

The Lord Christ died "that He might deliver us out of this present evil age" (Galatians 1:4, mg.); on the cross delivering us "*out of the power of darkness*" (Colossians 1:13)—from the "world-rulers of this darkness" (Ephesians 6:12)—and translating us "into the kingdom of the Son." We are therefore crucified to the world, not simply "worldly" things or ways but *to the world itself.* And, crucified with Christ, we must expect the world to look upon us as it looked upon Him when He hung upon the tree. Nailed there with Him, we too must look at the world *from* the cross, and with the spirit of the crucified Jesus pray for those who are nailing us to that cross.

That we may view the world in the light of the cross, let us once more go to the place called Calvary and see arrayed against the Holy One of God all the elements that go to make up this present evil world, and know what all who are united to Christ must *expect* if they are willing to suffer with Him that they may be also glorified with Him.

> "The soldiers when they had crucified Jesus, took His garments. . . . Let us . . . cast lots."—John 19:23–24.

In the four soldiers gambling at the foot of the cross we see that side of human nature which is callous to the sufferings of others and takes advantage of all who are in its power.

Alas, what multitudes today are represented by the executioners of the Christ. They cry, "Let us eat and drink, for tomorrow we die," and have no thought beyond the physical needs of the moment.

To souls who are responsive to the crucifixion and capable of feeling sensitively for others, what suffering it is to meet this element in this evil world. Alas for all who are in its power!

> "The chief priests mocking Him, with the scribes and elders, said, . . . Let Him now come down from the cross, and we will believe."—Matthew 27:41–42.

There is also a "religious" world which rejects the cross of Jesus: they who are not prepared to follow a crucified Lord; who "love the chief place" and the "chief seats," "and the salutations in the marketplaces, and to be called of men, Rabbi" (Matthew 23:6–7). They who "say and do not," and "all their works they do for to be seen of men" (Matthew 23:3–5). This religious world loves *not* the cross, even though in this twentieth century it bears the name of Him who died upon the cross! Love of power and the praise of men is contrary to the spirit of the cross.

> "They that passed by railed on Him, wagging their heads, and saying, Ha! Thou that destroyest the temple, and buildest it in three days, save Thyself, and come down from the cross."—Mark 15:29–30.

The mixed multitude pass by the cross and join in the general cry. They are but sheep led as a flock by the leaders of men. They sense the mind of their leaders and are quickly swayed by the spirit of the hour. They pass by the cross and rail on the crucified One, casting in His teeth the words that He had spoken. Soldiers and thieves, rulers, chief priests, elders and scribes, with all the multitude, were of one mind that awful day. Religious men, rough soldiers, criminals and men of the world, all forgot the barriers that separated them and joined together at Calvary. One united cry came from their lips: "*If*" He was the Christ, "*let Him save Himself.*" The cross appeared to them proof that he was NOT the Son of God. Let Him give supernatural signs and they would believe, they said. It was not too late to prove Himself the Messiah: "Let Him come down"—that was all!

So it is today. All the elements of this present evil world become united at Calvary. The fleshly element, the wise of the world, the criminal classes and traditional religionists join with the special forces of the evil one in the great revolt against the cross. And once again they who stand by the cross of Jesus are a little band, the very preaching of the cross marking them out as "crucified to the world." The cross becomes the instrument of their crucifixion as it was of His. The cross once again manifests its severing power. There is no neutral ground at Calvary.

Had we stood by the cross of Jesus that awful day, would we have cried "*The offense of the cross shall be my proudest boast*"? Will we *now* consent to take the cross and be ostracized by the world? Not only the *worldly world*—the world with its aims, its interests, its spirit of self-seeking, self-glorying and self-love—but even the *religious world,* in so far as the "elements of the world" are in it and it seeks to come between us and our Lord? "Jesus . . . suffered without the gate. Let us therefore go forth unto Him without the camp, bearing His reproach" (Hebrews 13:12–13).

THE ELEMENTS OF THE WORLD IN THE CHRISTIAN LIFE

> "If ye *died with Christ* from the elements of the world, why, as though living in the world . . . ?"
> —Colossians 2:20, mg.

The Galatian believers were in danger of going back to reliance upon works of law for growth in their Christian experience, but the Colossians were being drawn aside from Christ in another way—through "philosophy" and "tradition of men"—which Paul plainly said was "after the elements of the world, and not after Christ."

To both Galatians and Colossians Paul had the same message—*the message of Calvary.*

He would not add one more voice to the clamor in Colosse, for the Colossians were already perplexed enough with "precepts and doctrines of men"—various factions who were judging them in respect of "meat" and "drink" and feast days (Colossians 2:16). All these are external things which, under the old law, were a "*shadow of the things to come*" in Christ and are now of little importance. The apostle takes them back to Calvary and asks, "If you *died* with Christ, *why* are you acting as if you were still *living in the world*?"

Why do you go back to the "childish lessons of outward things" (Colossians 2:20, C.H.) and submit yourselves to the rule of others, who are "taking [their] stand upon the things . . . *seen,* vainly puffed up by [the] fleshly mind" (Colossians 2:18, mg.), and not holding fast to Christ, who is the Head of His Body, the Church, and is the life of His members, so that His Body increases from within, by a spontaneous life which is the very "increase of God" (Colossians 2:19)?

But if you have *died* with Christ, so that now you are joined to Him as your life, why go back to the ground of "Touch not" this or that? All these exterior things "perish with the using." "Food will not commend us to God: neither, if we eat not, are we the worse; nor, if we eat, are we the better" (1 Corinthians 8:8).

Paul admits that asceticism has a "show of wisdom," but it is, as far as commands from God go, a "*self-chosen worship*" (Colossians 2:23, C.H.). It has the appearance of "humility" and wise "severity to the body," but none of these things are "*of any value against the indulgence of the flesh*" (Colossians 2:23).

Paul declares that the Colossians had *died* with Christ from all these elements of the world—elements which were "after the tradition of men," the outcome of "vain deceit" in men's minds. Why were they then imagining that by such observances they could conquer themselves? This was not following Christ. In Him was the *true* circumcision (Colossians 2:11)—the circumcision of the *heart.*

They were buried with Him in His grave and quickened with Him to a *new* life; therefore they were not to act as if they were now *"living in the world."*

Crucified with Christ, they were *"raised together with Christ,"* and a heart belief of this would bring in a supernatural power—the power of Christ's resurrection. Instead of being occupied therefore with cutting off exterior things, and questioning whether they should do this or that, they should have been seeking the things above and setting their mind on the heavenly fullness which was theirs in Christ (Colossians 3:1–3).

"For ye *died,"* repeats the apostle, *"and your life is hid with Christ in God"* (Colossians 3:3). They were *severed* from the old life to share the life of Christ; and through this life from God they could *"make dead"* their "members" (Colossians 3:5, mg.) and learn the secret of deliverance from the indulgence of the flesh.

The dangers that assailed the Colossian believers are ours today, ofttimes under the name of holiness or consecration. So let us beware.

Worldly Christians (what a contradiction of terms!) are not so liable to these special snares, but those who long to follow the Lord can be quickly influenced by the "precepts of men," especially those of men whom they esteem very highly in love for their work's sake. The *cross of Christ* is the message, and it is the remedy for all. Let us truly consent with all our hearts to be crucified with Him and it will not be long before we find that the world is crucified to *us*. It will have lost its power to attract or, in its religious aspect, to influence us in our walk before the Lord.

All that is "in the world; the lust [desire] of the flesh, and the [desire] of the eyes, and the vainglory of life"—all that is "*not of the Father, but is of the world*" (1 John 2:16)—will be crucified to us, and we shall overcome the world, because greater is He that is in us than "he that is in the world" (1 John 4:4).

THE CROSS AS THE BASIS OF UNITY

> "We are made nigh in the blood of Christ. For He is our peace, who made both one . . . and . . . reconciled them both in one body unto God

> through the cross, having slain the enmity thereby."—Ephesians 2:13–16.

If the cross of Calvary is the severing power between the child of God and the world, it is equally the uniting power between all who draw nigh to God through the precious blood.

It is on the *life* side of the cross that the blood-bought children of God most clearly realize the oneness of all who are "in Christ Jesus." The message of Calvary is preached to the sinner as the ground of reconciliation with God, but it should also be emphatically proclaimed as the ground of unity between man and man, even between the professing followers of Christ.

How sorely we need to see that all divisions between true children of God are part of those "elements of the world" to which they have died with the crucified Lord; and so far as we tolerate anything in our lives from which Christ died to deliver us, so far is there a "practical denial of the efficacy of Christ's death" (Lightfoot).

Paul the apostle, who had once been a member of the most exclusive caste of the Hebrews, clearly saw that the death of Christ had broken down all walls of partition between men who sought to worship the same Lord. And so, with the same intensity that he once sought to stamp out the followers of the despised Nazarene, he abandoned himself to the claims of the Crucified One and with no uncertain sound preached "the faith which he once destroyed" (Galatians 1:23, A.V.).

The "word of the cross" revolutionized his life; it swept away his preconceived ideas, his national prejudices, his pride of race, his exclusive caste.

The cross as the gateway into a new life is Paul's constant theme, and writing to the Colossians he impresses upon them that they have died with Him who died, henceforth to live in a new sphere where the distinctions and divisions of earth have no place—"where there cannot be Greek and Jew, circumcision and uncircumcision, barbarian, Scythian, bondman, freeman; but Christ is all and in all" (Colossians 3:11).

"In one Spirit were we all baptized into one body, whether Jews or Greeks, whether bond or free" (1 Corinthians 12:13), he writes again to the Corinthians.

The Jews called the Gentiles the "Uncircumcision," and the barrier between them consisted of this outward rite as well as the Mosaic law and the Levitical sacrifices—all ordained by God until Christ Himself would come as fulfillment of all these observances and as the one complete and sufficient sacrifice for the sins of the people.

Paul says that Christ "abolished in His flesh the enmity, even the law of commandments contained in ordinances" (Ephesians 2:15), and Himself became the peace, for out of Jew and Gentile He would create of the twain "*one new man*." For Jew and Gentile, *as* Jew and Gentile, *died* with Him. If they draw nigh to God through Him, Jew and Gentile will be reconciled unto God and made into a new entity, the Body of Christ. So it was through His cross that He slew the enmity between them.

Oh glorious message of Calvary, out of which the Christian Church has sprung, and all the blessings of freedom which we enjoy in the twentieth century; for through the cross of Calvary, so marvelously illumined to Paul the apostle by the risen Lord Himself, and made clear by Paul's own faithful preaching of the cross, we Gentiles have become *"fellow-heirs," "fellow-members," "fellow-partakers,"* of the promise in Jesus Christ through the gospel (Ephesians 3:6).

And yet even now in the professing Christian Church, called by the name of Christ, are to be seen many barriers between worshipers of God resembling those that stood between Jew and Gentile in the days of Paul!

"He came and preached good tidings of peace" (Ephesians 2:17, mg.), writes Paul to the Ephesians. The Risen One, with the marks of His passion in His hands—He who died to create out of all the races of men "one new man"—comes Himself with the message of peace. Oh that He may come again to His people today with the same glad tidings, showing to us His hands and His side, and saying:

> "Peace be unto you,"
>
> uniting all the sections of the living members of His Church, "THROUGH THE CROSS"!

CHAPTER 10

"To this end was the Son of God manifested, that He might destroy the works of the devil."

—1 John 3:8.

THE CROSS AND THE POWERS OF DARKNESS

"He blotted out the handwriting of our debts . . . affixed [it] to His cross. And, by yielding up His body, He showed contempt for principalities and authorities; and put them to shame, openly, in His own Person."

—Colossians 2:14–15, Syriac Version.

ANOTHER aspect of the work of Christ upon the cross of Calvary comes before us here. By His death He "despoiled the principalities and the powers," and "made a show of them openly, triumphing over them in it [or, in Himself]," writes Paul to the Colossians.

These principalities and powers are described in Ephesians 6:12 as the "world-rulers of this darkness," wicked spirits—or "spiritual hosts of wickedness"—in high or heavenly places.

The victory of the cross was especially mentioned by Isaiah when he foretold that the Man of sorrows would "divide the spoil with the strong"; and now Paul the apostle proclaims that on the cross the Lord Christ despoiled the principalities and powers and triumphed over them.

Once again we notice the clear vision of all that was accomplished at Calvary and given to souls on the resurrection side of the cross. It is not until the believer apprehends his death with Christ as well as Christ's death for him that he actually passes into the sphere which Paul describes as the "heavenlies," where he lives "in the Spirit" and walks "after the Spirit."

In this sphere he realizes the actual existence of the forces of darkness described by the apostle, for they are "spiritual" hosts unknown by those who walk "after the flesh," who are "yet carnal" and live "according to men" (1 Corinthians 3:3).

It is therefore to the interest of the "world-rulers of this darkness" that the children of God should not understand the twofold message of Calvary through which they enter the sphere where their eyes are opened to the wiles of the devil, and where they see that their "wrestling is not against flesh and blood, but against the . . . spiritual hosts of wickedness" (Ephesians 6:12).

It is true that the adversary of souls resists the message of the cross in every aspect, but all the powers of hell are aroused to prevent the believer's knowledge of the victory of Calvary over the prince of darkness and his evil hosts. On the earthward side of the cross, the subtle foe ofttimes persuades even true children of God that he does not exist at all. Or, going to the other extreme, he magnifies his power and holds them in slavery to habits of sin, deluding them into belief that there is no deliverance on this side of the grave.

In their service for God many Christians are wielding carnal weapons, of no avail against the real foe. Others are filled with earnest plans and labor with heart and soul to win the masses to their Lord. But in both cases, behind and around them is the evil one and his real but unseen hosts of wickedness, who laugh at every weapon of the flesh and fear nothing but the power of the finished work of Christ when manifested by the Holy Spirit through men and women who have become in very truth crucified messengers of a crucified Lord.

Since this is so, we do not marvel that the prince of darkness hates the cross, spares no effort to nullify its message, hides its full meaning from the children of God, and hesitates at nothing to keep them from knowing its power.

Fully aware of the prophecy of Isaiah that the Man of Calvary would take "the prey from the terrible" and "divide the spoil with the strong" by pouring out His soul unto death, the "terrible one" himself came to the Christ of God when He walked on earth and tried his utmost to keep Him from the cross. In the wilderness he offered Him all the kingdoms of this world, without the necessity of going to the cross, if He would but bow down to him. But with His face set as flint to accomplish His Father's will, Christ answers, "It is written, Thou shalt worship the Lord thy God," and turns from the tempter toward the cross of shame.

The temptation was renewed later through the lips of His disciple Peter when he urges the Master to "pity Himself," as he hears from Him of His prospective sufferings and death. "Get thee behind me, *Satan*," said the Lord. "Thou art a stumbling-block unto Me: for thou mindest not the things of God, but the things of men" (see Matthew 16:23).

Satan is baffled once more, and leaves the Son of God "but for a season" before renewing his attacks again and again. He raged against Him through the demons who possessed the bodies of men, for all "wicked spirits" knew that this Holy One of God would end their authority and power over men.

At last the final conflict is at hand. The adversary has failed to turn the Christ from the cross and now becomes the bitter instigator of it.

The words of the Son of God as He drew nigh to the time of His sufferings show that

He clearly knew the purpose of His death. It was to be not only "a ransom for all" but a final and complete triumph over the powers of hell. "Now shall the prince of this world be cast out. And I, if I be lifted up out of the earth, will draw all men unto Myself" (John 12:31–32, mg.), said the Lord to His disciples, foretelling the power that would be centered in Calvary to draw souls unto Himself, out of the death of sin and the captivity of the devil.

At the supper table again the Lord said, "The prince of this world cometh, but he hath nothing in Me" (John 14:30–31). For He loved the Father, and as He gave Him commandment to go to the cross, even so He would do. He would lay down His life of His own free choice, to save the sheep from the wolf who had snatched them from their God.

Failing utterly in his attempt to keep the Son of God from the cross, the prince of darkness enters into one of the Master's own disciples to lead Him to the cross.

At the supper table the devil "put into the heart of Judas" (John 13:2) the awful thought of betraying Him; and after he had taken bread from the very hand of Christ, "then entered

Satan into him," and he hastens away to fulfill the behests of the archenemy of his Lord.

Oh solemn fact, that the spirit of evil must find human beings to carry out his plans even as the Holy Spirit of God seeks yielded hearts and lives to fulfill the counsels of God.

"This is your hour, and the power of darkness" (Luke 22:53), said the Christ later, when, in the garden of Gethsemane, after His agony even unto blood, they seized Him and led Him to the judgment hall. From this moment He was given over to the world-rulers of this darkness, who were permitted to exercise their power upon Him to the full, and by the hands of wicked men through whom they worked their will, they "killed the Prince of life."

THE HOUR OF TRIUMPH

> "Having despoiled the principalities and the powers, He made a show of them openly, triumphing over them in it."—Colossians 2:15.

This is the tragedy of Calvary described from the divine standpoint.

At the moment when, before the eyes of the world, the prince of the world succeeded in putting to open shame and humiliation the Christ of God, triumphing over His body even unto death . . . at that same moment, before God and the hosts of heaven, principalities and powers were *themselves* put to shame and triumphed over by the Christ they crucified!

Paul says these evil forces were "displayed," "as a victor displays his captives or trophies in a triumphal procession" (Lightfoot). The Conqueror was, so to speak, "leading them in triumph" before the hosts of heaven. The metaphor used is similar to the one found in 2 Corinthians 2:14, but there Christ leads in triumph those who are conquered by His love and who gladly become the trophies of His death.

What a picture is here before us of the victory of Calvary! What a contrast to the scene on earth is now presented! The mocking multitude around the cross little knew of the triumphal procession in the unseen realm, when all the hosts of evil were put to open shame by their Conqueror.

The apostle, in such a picture, places "the paradox of the crucifixion in the strongest light. . . . The convict's gibbet is the Victor's car" (Lightfoot).

THE TESTIMONY OF THE HOLY SPIRIT

> "The Comforter . . . will convict . . . of judgment, because the prince of this world hath been judged."—John 16:7–11.

On the eve of His cross and passion, the Lord told His disciples of the coming of the Spirit of truth to dwell in them, to bear witness to Him and glorify Him.

Before the cross the Lord had said, "Now is the prince of this world cast out," but after His death and resurrection the testimony of the Spirit would be "the prince of this world *hath been* judged" (John 16:11).

The Son of God accomplished the victory over the powers of hell upon the cross of Calvary, and the Holy Spirit is given to convince the world of the victory and bear witness to the work of the Son of God.

Yet how few of the children of God realize that, through the death on Calvary, the adversary of their souls is a *conquered* foe! How few know how to meet the wiles of the evil one, and yet fewer how to attack him in aggressive warfare and participate in the triumphs of the cross!

THE BLOOD OF THE LAMB

> "They overcame him because of the blood of the Lamb, and because of the word of their testimony; and they loved not their life even unto death."—Revelation 12:11.

In this chapter of the Apocalypse, the veil is drawn aside for a moment to show the conflict in the unseen world. Whether it speaks prophetically of some special time in the future is immaterial for us now to consider. It is at least clear that, just as there was a final conflict on the cross between the Prince of life and the prince of darkness, when the latter was cast down from his place of authority over all who would trust in the Crucified One, so there will be a final conflict in the heavens, when the hosts of the Lord will come forth to cast the dragon and his angels down to the earth, whence they will finally go into the pit and then into the lake of fire.

But the dragon and his angels are still at large! Though the principalities and powers were conquered on the cross of Calvary, there is an interval between that glorious triumph and the time of their final casting down—an interval during which each redeemed soul must appropriate the victory of Calvary and individually overcome the conquered foe, and thus win the crown with those overcomers who will share the Victor's throne.

In this unveiling of the final conflict in the heavens, we are shown the threefold secret of victory and the way in which each overcomer triumphs over the foe.

"They overcame him *because of the blood of the Lamb*." This takes us back to Calvary and the sufferings of the Christ. These overcomers had manifestly been taught by the Holy Spirit the victory of the cross; the blood—or death—of the Lamb was, therefore, the one weapon they used against the foe.

This was accompanied by *"the word of their testimony"*—a fearless confession of Christ. *"And they loved not their life even unto death"*—they not only wielded the power of the cross for victory over the evil one but they had "drunk in" the spirit of Him who died and consequently lived the crucified life, triumphing over the prince of darkness through the Spirit of their Lord. The *cross* is the way of victory for all the children of God. United to the Lord in His death, they share His risen life and are seated with Him in the heavenlies, "far above all" the principalities and powers of hell.

THE CRUCIFIXION

> "Forasmuch then as Christ suffered in the flesh, arm ye yourselves also with the same mind."—1 Peter 4:1.

The adversary may be a conquered foe; the power of the blood may be ready for us to wield in the hour of conflict; but unless we seek to know in ever deeper measure the inner spirit of the crucified Jesus, we shall still be powerless in the fight with the forces of evil attacking us.

"Christ suffered in the flesh," writes the apostle Peter, so "arm ye yourselves with the same mind." The Lord Jesus deliberately chose the path of suffering in this present evil world. He deliberately took the place of weakness, "becoming in the likeness of men" although He was Almighty; deliberately humbled Himself as a man by going to the lowest point of humiliation earth could find for Him, although in heaven He was on an equality with God; deliberately followed the path of obedience to God's will, even until it led Him to a cross of agony and shame. Step by step, lower and lower He went. The cross was no theory to Him! He *suffered* in the flesh.

Oh child of God, arm yourself with the same mind. Let this mind be in you which was in Christ Jesus. If you will choose that the spirit of His death on the cross shall be imparted to you, you will "cease unto sins" (1 Peter 4:1, mg.) and no longer live according to the usual desires of the natural man but according to the contrary standpoint of the "will of God."

It is true that others will "think it strange" and may "speak evil of you," but "if ye be reproached for . . . Christ, happy are ye; for the Spirit of glory and of God resteth upon you: on their part He is evil spoken of, but on your part He is glorified" (1 Peter 4:14, A.V.).

We must be armed within by the inbreathed crucifixion spirit of Jesus if we are to triumph without, wield with certain victory the weapon of the "blood of the Lamb," and prove through personal experience that on Calvary the devil became a conquered foe.

THE WHOLE ARMOR OF GOD

> "Put on the whole armor of God, that ye may be able to stand against the wiles of the devil . . . and, having overcome all, to stand."—Ephesians 6:11–13, mg.

Paul here most vividly describes the enemy and the conflict into which we emerge on the resurrection side of Calvary.

"Be made powerful in the Lord," writes Paul, "and in the strength of His might" (Ephesians 6:10, mg.). This presupposes that the believer has come to an end of his own might, for it is to those who have been "quickened with Christ" and "raised up with Him" and made to "sit with Him in the heavenly places in Christ Jesus" (Ephesians 2:5–6)—thus putting on "the new man" (Ephesians 4:24)—that the apostle writes.

How are they to act in the hour of fierce temptation is the question in their hearts. They have been "crucified with Christ," and now, moment by moment living by His life, are they to fight? Or what are they to do?

They are to be "powerful *in the Lord*," and strengthened by His might in them they are just to stand their ground! Stand against all the "wiles of the devil" (v. 11) to get them away from Calvary and their place "in the Lord."

"For our wrestling is not against flesh and blood" (v. 12), writes Paul. "Wrestling"—yes, the spiritual enemy attacks the spiritual man in a spiritual way, and the believer is conscious of a hand-to-hand conflict with some unseen foe, who, so to speak, winds himself around the inner man and "wrestles" in very truth. To "fight" is hopeless; the believer can only "stand firm" (Conybeare) and refuse at all costs to surrender his position in Christ or yield to the wiles of the devil.

The reference to "flesh and blood" suggests that these "wiles" often come in human guise! But the soul strongly entrenched in the Lord is given acute vision to discern "the spirit that now worketh in the sons of disobedience" (Ephesians 2:2), yes, but ofttimes also by means of servants of God—as we have seen he did through Peter to tempt the Son of God and when Satan moved David to act without the commands of God.

Strengthened with power by the Holy Spirit in the inner man, the believer becomes a true warrior of God, increasingly able to recognize the principalities and powers as the "world-rulers of this darkness," and learns that the "prince of the power of the air" (Ephesians 2:2) has resources in the forces of the air to attack the child of God as he attacked Job, and is able to move men as tools to fulfill his will, even without their knowledge.

"Wherefore, take up with you to the battle the whole armor of God" (Ephesians 6:13, Conybeare), cries the warrior Paul. The Christ has nullified these spiritual hosts of wickedness in His triumph at the cross, but you who are joined to Him must actively and ceaselessly "take up" the armor thus provided for you.

Christ has not triumphed at the cost of His life to give you nothing to do, O child of God. You have *your* part in the conflict; you must overcome as He overcame if you are to share His Throne.

When you learn the victory of Calvary and hasten out of yourself *into Christ*, host after host will come up against you and seek to draw you out from your Lord. That you may "withstand them in the evil day" (Conybeare) you must see to it that you have taken by the hand of faith every part of the armor of God.

If you will put on the whole armor, you shall "withstand," and "having overthrown them all" (Conybeare)—all the spirits of evil that will swarm around you with innumerable wiles—you shall stand unshaken, victorious through the blood of the Lamb.

The "whole armor" is the Lord Christ Himself. You dwell "in the Lord," and "in Him" you must "be made powerful" to meet all the hosts of hell.

If you will abide in Him you must take heed to be "girt with the belt of truth" (Conybeare), for one shade of anything in your life that is contrary to truth, before the eyes of Him who is the Truth, will bring complete defeat at the hands of the foe.

The breastplate of righteousness will be yours while you truly abide in Him who is your right-eousness and do not allow anything in your life contrary to the righteousness of Him whose scepter is a scepter of uprightness indeed (Hebrews 1:8).

"In the Lord" you must be a ready messenger of the glad tidings of peace, for you are "saved to serve," and you must with alacrity obey the promptings of the Spirit as you walk the earth or you will give occasion to your watchful foe.

You must quickly take, and hide behind, the "shield of faith" from the "fiery darts of the evil one," and especially keep the "helmet of salvation" upon your head, lest by any means, as the serpent beguiled Eve in his craftiness, your "thoughts" should be corrupted from the "simplicity that is in Christ" (2 Corinthians 11:3). Above all, for defense and attack, you will ceaselessly need the sword of the Spirit, the Word of God, which is living and active, and sharper than any two-edged sword.

In intimate converse with your Lord, speaking to Him at "all seasons in the Spirit" (Ephesians 6:18), you shall be equipped to meet the foe, and be more than conqueror through Him who loves you.

Knowing also the fierceness of the fight—and that when one member of the Body of Christ suffers, all suffer too—you will with "all perseverance" be pleading for "all saints," especially on the behalf of those who, like the warrior Paul, are in the front lines of the battle of the Lord.

Then you shall be taught by Him how to "stand in the battle in the day of the Lord," and will be sent forth as an armed warrior, clothed in shining armor, in aggressive warfare to win the trophies of the cross, seeing signs and wonders done in the name of the crucified and risen Lord.

CHAPTER 11

"If we died with Him, we shall also live with Him; if we endure, we shall also reign with Him."

—2 Timothy 2:11–12.

THE CROSS AND ITS CONTINUITY

"That I may know Him, and the power of His resurrection, and the fellowships of His sufferings, becoming conformed unto His death."

—Philippians 3:10.

ONCE more we meet with the words "*His death*," and this time in the letter of Paul to his beloved Philippians.

The epistle was written some six years after the letter to the Galatians, when Paul so exultingly cries, "I *have been* crucified with Christ." Yet here we find him speaking of an assimilation with, or conformity to, the death of Christ as the condition of knowing in greater power the efficacy of Christ's resurrection.

In all the Scriptures we can find no clearer evidence of the *continuity* of the cross in the Christian life.

Paul had clearly and unmistakably known the fullness of the Holy Spirit; he had been commissioned—and given his message of the cross—by direct revelation from Christ Himself; he had plainly preached deliverance from the bondage of sin through the cross; and in his letter to the Roman Christians he had explained the identity of the believer with the Lord in His death and the mighty, effectual working of the Spirit of life in Christ to make the believer free from the law of sin and death.

Yet, with all this behind him as a message sealed by the power of the Holy Spirit and personally experienced in his own life, we still have the apostle seeking to know *more* of "His death."

A manifestly deeper stratum of experience is revealed in Paul's words here, and they clearly show that *fuller maturity* in the spiritual life means *deeper fellowship with the sufferings of Christ,* for "the climax of the risen life gravitates, strange to say, back to the cross" (C.A. Fox).

The apostle therefore presses on toward "the prize of the upward calling of God in Christ Jesus" by eagerly desiring to be made conformable unto the death of his Lord, since he knew that to "suffer with Him" is also to be "glorified together" (Romans 8:17, A.V.) with Him.

Let us turn to the letters of the apostle and see in his own life what conformity to the cross means in actual experience.

THE SENTENCE OF DEATH

> "Weighed down exceedingly. . . ."
>
> "Beyond our power. . . ."
>
> "Despaired even of life. . . ."
>
> "The sentence of *death* . . . that we should not trust in ourselves, but in God who raiseth the dead."—2 Corinthians 1:8–9.

It is clear from this passage that however fully we may apprehend our death with Christ and know the power of His resurrection, we are brought again and again to a place where we realize, not only as an admitted principle but *in actual fact*, that we have no strength or resources of our own.

"*We despaired even of life,*" writes Paul, but we had the answer from God that it was "death within ourselves," so that we might be brought to such despair as to be compelled to cast ourselves upon Him who alone can raise the dead. He delivered us in our extreme need, and on Him we have set our hope that He will still deliver.

This is the meaning of the many afflictions which befall the soul who has joyfully cried, "I have been crucified with Christ." We must learn how to *prove* the power of the God who raises the dead, by being brought to our wit's end and to place after place where circumstances are beyond our power and we are in utter despair of all help but in God.

Since Paul the apostle could thus write of himself after all *he* had known of God, to "trust in ourselves" is undoubtedly a danger to us all our life long; and to be kept *at an end of ourselves* is evidently a necessity for the manifestation of the resurrection power of Christ.

CRUCIFIED THROUGH WEAKNESS

> "He was crucified through weakness . . . we also are *weak with Him*."—2 Corinthians 13:4, mg.

In these words we have another aspect of "*being made conformable to His death*." The human weakness of Christ when He permitted Himself to be led as a lamb to the slaughter, as a victim weak and powerless in the hands of men, was to Paul a picture of his own weakness.

He looks at the Son of God "crucified through weakness" and cries, "*I also am weak with Him*"; but again he thinks of the Christ "raised by the glory of the Father," and remembering how He "lived through the power of God," rejoicingly knows that even in his weakness he, too, may share the life of Christ by the same mighty energizing power of God. And so he adds, "I shall *live* with Him *by the power of God towards you*." I am weak in myself, cries Paul. I, too, am "crucified" by my weakness, but made conformable to the death of my Lord; so I count upon His *life* to work in me, and *through me toward you Corinthians*. In dealing with you I shall prove *not my weakness* but the divine power of Christ speaking in me. I am weak, it is true, but *He* is not weak through me; He is *powerful in you*.

"Crucified through weakness" is then one aspect of the "being made conformable to His death." Yet how many think that they must *feel* power in themselves, or must become, so to speak, reservoirs of power or surcharged batteries of heavenly "dunamis"!

We are sorely hindered by our human conceptions of these heavenly mysteries, yet the divine ideal of power is revealed in the silent suffering Man on the way to Calvary! "The weakness of God" is "stronger than men," but it is so contrary to the human conception of power that we need to have our eyes opened by the Holy Spirit to see the pattern. And we need the imparting of the same Spirit to even create in us the *desire* to be conformed to the likeness set before us, and then to fulfill it in us by the same power.

"*Conformity to His death*" on the resurrection side of the cross means a deepening weakness in ourselves, not an increasing sense of strength! It is a weakness that is truly a crucifixion, because it is so contrary to our natural desire to *feel* we *can* do this or that. But to be kept consciously weak and yet to walk by faith, drawing upon the divine strength—*by faith* to act upon the power of God, *by faith* to count upon "Christ speaking in me," *by faith* to "live with Him" by the power of God toward *others* rather than toward ourselves—is a life of faith indeed.

"*Weakness, fear, and much trembling*" in the believer, accompanied by the "demonstration of the Spirit and power" in the hearts and lives of others, is God's way of manifesting the life of Christ through those who are crucified with Him.

THE DYING JESUS

> "Always bearing about in the body the dying of Jesus, that the life also of Jesus may be manifested in our body."—2 Corinthians 4:10.

Once more we get a glimpse of Paul's deep insight into Calvary and see how the death and risen life of Jesus is interwoven with all his thoughts, and is ever to him the basis of all advancement in the spiritual life. It is well always to place this passage by the side of the sixth chapter of the Epistle to the Romans, for one is the outcome of the other. 2 Corinthians 4:10 describes the subjective outcome of the objective sight of the work of Christ on Calvary, and without this subjective working in the believer of the "putting to death of Jesus" there cannot be the increasing manifestation in power of the life of Jesus through us in the world around.

Many know the truth of identification with Christ in death and have seen themselves as crucified with Him, and in the joy of their fresh vision and faith they have gone forth to service in dependence upon the risen Lord. For a time there is the seal of God on their testimony, but gradually the life ceases to flow in power and their witness becomes hollow and empty as a tinkling cymbal—alas, too often unconsciously to themselves.

What is the matter? They are living upon a *past experience of the deliverance of the cross*, and have failed to see that after the objective vision of Calvary and their identification with Christ in His death, *death must still be the basis of ever- increasing life* all the way; for "always bearing about in the body the dying of Jesus" is the unvarying condition for the continual manifestation of His life.

What the "putting to death" (A.S.V. mg.) of Jesus in the experience of the child of God practically means, the context of the passage shows. The Christ upon His cross was pressed on every side, but not crushed in His power to endure; He was perplexed over the withdrawal of His Father's face, and cried, "Why hast Thou forsaken Me?" yet He was not in despair; He was pursued by all the forces of darkness, yet He was not forsaken by God, who sustained Him to the end; He was smitten down to death, yet not destroyed, for He lived by the power of God.

Even so was Paul pressed, perplexed, pursued, and smitten down. But always true to the principle of the cross which had been revealed to him by Christ, he sees that in all his sufferings he was but "*bearing about . . . the dying of Jesus*" so that the life of Jesus might be manifested in his mortal body. He was kept at an end of all power in himself so that the power which energized him might wholly be of God.

Thus does the All-wise Lord deal with His children to keep them truly dependent upon Him, and really empty vessels for His use. Thus does He *press out all strength and power of their own* to cause them to draw all their strength alone from Him. The Lord knows how to bring them into circumstances where only His life can carry them through; into places where the pressure on every side calls forth the boundless resources of God; where they walk in a maze of perplexity, but afterwards find how truly His skillful hands have guided them; where they are tossed to and fro in a stormy sea, but are not forsaken by God; where they are "smitten down," and apparently all things are against them, and yet find that the life of Jesus is manifested through them in its power of divine endurance, to the glory of His grace.

ALWAYS DELIVERED TO DEATH

> "For we which live are always delivered unto death for Jesus' sake, that the life also of Jesus may be manifested in our mortal flesh."—2 Corinthians 4:11.

This verse seems at first sight to be simply a repetition of the previous one. But in "words which the Holy Spirit teacheth" every change of sentence has its meaning, and there is a difference here which seems to point to a still deeper conformity to death, this time for *Jesus' sake*.

The concluding sentence of the paragraph which begins with verse 7 plainly tells us that at first "always bearing about the dying of Jesus" is for our *own* sake, that we may be kept at the point where we have no power of our own to draw upon and the exceeding greatness of the power may be proved to be of *God* and not from ourselves.

But now the believer thus kept at an end of himself, and living by the life of Jesus manifested in the body of clay, is further, and deliberately, *"delivered unto death for Jesus' sake." Delivered* unto weakness upon weakness, trial after trial, perplexity after perplexity, conflict after conflict— all for the sake of Him who died that *He* might see of the travail of His soul and be satisfied.

Are we children of God willing for fellowship with our Lord to this extent? Have we not rather borne trial after trial in the hope that a point would come where we would realize nought but "glory to glory" in the spiritual life?

But how little we have understood the law of sacrifice for fruitfulness. Joined to the Living One, we will be led on until the true light of life in Him dawns upon us and our clouded idea of divine things passes away. We need to see that we are in truth led from "glory to glory" in the light of His face *that we may be enabled to bear still deeper fellowship with Him as the One who died,* and fill up that which is lacking in the afflictions of Christ for His Church's sake (Colossians 1:24).

DEATH WORKETH FOR LIFE IN OTHERS

> "So then *death* worketh *in us,* but *life in you.*"—2 Corinthians 4:12.

This is the outcome of being delivered to death for Jesus' sake. Death works in us for the fruit of life in *others.*

We may desire to be used and to win souls, but is our desire strong enough for this? Strong enough to pour out our life for others and have nothing but emptiness and weakness for ourselves! This is real self-sacrifice; real selflessness; real self-effacement. This is the true spirit of the cross, and the true manifestation of the life of Jesus in mortal flesh; for this is the very love of Christ which impelled Him to Calvary, where He had nought but the death with all its unspeakable horror and shame that we might have the life from God through Him.

There is only one way to really win souls, and this is the *way of sacrifice.* It cost the Christ His life on Calvary, and, in union with Him it must cost our lives also if we are to be the channels of His life to others.

If we know the cross in its true inward power in the very depths of our being, so will the depths of other hearts be touched and the life-power work within them, for just so far as the *death works in us,* so far will the *life* quicken souls around—souls "for whom Christ died."

This is the apostolic life that each of the redeemed may know—the life of fruitfulness. This is the "fatherhood" referred to by Paul when he said, "In Christ Jesus I begat you through the gospel." There are still "ten thousand tutors," but "*not many fathers.*" Not many who are willing to know that conformity to death which brings the travail for souls, in fellowship with Him who travailed on Calvary's cross for us.

"Death worketh in us," writes Paul. It is remarkable that the eighth chapter of the Epistle to the Romans, with its full and glorious gospel of freedom by the Spirit of life in Christ, its unveiling of the gladness of access to the Father, its exposition of the witness of the indwelling Spirit and our heirship in union with Christ, concludes with a striking description of the conformity to *death* which is the outward accompaniment of it all.

"For Thy sake we are killed all the day long . . . accounted as sheep for the slaughter" (Romans 8:36), cries Paul. But we are "more than conquerors through Him that loved us" is the triumphant testimony of the apostle. Yes, Christ was led as a lamb to the slaughter, and as we have chosen His cross and accounted ourselves as slaughtered with Him, should it be a disconcerting matter if others take the same view of us as we have taken of ourselves and account *us* as sheep for the slaughter too?

Oh children of God, we may preach the cross, and even fight for the cross, but we render void our very message unless we are prepared to *live the cross*, and, in Paul's language, be ready to be "killed all the day long," that thereby death shall work in us and life in others, to the glory of Him who for our sakes died and rose again.

"*So then* death worketh in us, but life in you," writes the apostle. *In us*—emptiness, weakness, suffering, pressure, perplexity, but *in you*—LIFE.

Even so, Father, for thus it seems good in Thy sight. Be it unto me according to Thy word.

CHAPTER 12

"He that overcometh, I will give to him to sit down with me in My throne, as I also overcame."

—Revelation 3:21.

THE CALL TO THE CROSS

"He that doth not take his cross and follow after Me is not worthy of Me."

—Matthew 10:38.

EARLY in His ministry the Saviour cried, "Take up your cross and follow Me," but He did not explain what taking the cross meant until He Himself had passed through death into the life beyond the tomb and ascended to His place on the right hand of the Majesty on high. From there, through His chosen vessel the apostle Paul, He interprets His cross and its claims upon all who desire to follow Him.

It is significant that Paul never says *take* your cross, but proclaims the cross of Christ as a cross which has *already triumphed* and bids the believer enter into the triumph of his Lord.

The words of *Paul* interpret the call to the cross given by the Lamb on the way to the cross, and the words of the *Christ* interpret again the message of Paul. Although the cross has already triumphed and the work of deliverance and victory over the powers of hell is already accomplished, yet believers must individually accept the cross in its experiential aspect and deliberately choose to follow the Lamb in His path of the cross on earth.

The call to the cross from the lips of Him who endured the cross still comes to each of His redeemed, and it foreshadows the only possible path in the present world for every follower of the Lamb.

Five times in the Gospels is the Lord's call to the cross recorded, and each time it unveils a different aspect of the cross in the believer's life when the call is truly obeyed.

Let us note first from the Master's words that—

THE PATH OF THE CROSS IS INEVITABLE

> "Whosoever doth not bear his own cross, and come after Me, *cannot* be My disciple."—Luke 14:27.

The path of the cross was inevitable for the Christ. To Nicodemus He said that "as Moses lifted up the serpent . . . even so *must* the Son of Man be lifted up" (John 3:14), and to the disciples, that He *must* go to Jerusalem and suffer and be killed. The "*must*" was imperative. "Thus it *must* be," He said at another time. He *must* lay down His life for the sheep and *must* bring them back to His Father (John 10:16–18).

But the path is the same for the Lamb *and* His followers. The "*must*" is as imperative for them as for Him, for did He not say that he who refuses to follow Him to the cross cannot be His disciple? Since the Christ took the cross in the sinner's stead to redeem him, he who would learn of Christ must take the cross of Christ or he cannot be taught by Him.

Until that time when the Lord Jesus began to show unto His disciples the path that lay before Him, they did not know what following Him would involve. They had heard His initial call and had left all to follow Him, believing that He was the Christ—as Peter confessed one day—for they knew in their hearts that He spoke the words of eternal life. They had seen His mighty works and marveled at His grace. But a *cross*! Suffering and death? No such thought had come to them. "But while all were marveling at the things which He did, He said unto His disciples, Let these words sink into your ears: *for the Son of Man shall be delivered into the hands of men. But they understood not*" (Luke 9:43–45).

It is thus with many children of God today, but with a difference. They know that Christ has borne the cross and that they have life through His death, but that He bore a cross *which must be their cross also* has not been thought of by them. They have not realized that the crucified Lord must have crucified followers, and a true following of the Lamb can only be through death, for the Lamb can only go one way on earth—the way of being led to the slaughter. It is only in *heaven* that a throne is given to a slain Lamb.

THE MEANING OF THE CROSS

> "If any man would come after Me, let him *deny* himself, and take up his cross and follow Me."—Matthew 16:24.

Let him deny *himself*! Not deny *pleasant things* to himself; nor even deny the *sins* of himself. But *deny himself*, and all that is bound up *in himself*—himself as the central source or cause of action; himself as the central object of all things which come to him from without!

Himself! Any other word would have narrowed the Lord's meaning of the cross, for it covers the whole of the deliverance of Calvary, as was afterwards revealed by the risen Lord to the apostle Paul. The crucial message of Calvary to man is salvation from "himself"! If he will take for himself the cross and, accepting the spirit of the cross as manifested in the Christ who died for him, *deny*—or *renounce*—*himself* as crucified on the cross with his Lord, he will in so doing be delivered from the bondage of his sins, the terror of the law, and the spirit of the world . . . as well as the power of the devil.

Oh blessed gospel of Calvary! How simple, how deep, how effective, how wise, for "*himself*" is the center and core of all the trouble, rebellion, selfishness, pride and sin! Let a man look at himself as nailed to the cross; day by day *deny*—or refuse to know—himself; and calmly, quietly, take the path of the cross, and he will follow the Lamb not only to Calvary but right to the center of heaven and share His throne.

THE DEPTH OF THE CROSS

> "Deny himself, and take up his cross. . . . For whosoever would save his life [soul, mg.] shall lose it."—Matthew 16:24–25.

Three times the Lord follows His call to the cross with mysterious words, unintelligible to the natural man and to the believer who walks "according to men." "Whosoever would save his life shall lose it; but *whosoever shall lose his life . . . shall save it*" (Luke 9:24). Again, when speaking not of the cross but of the grain of wheat falling into the ground to die, the Lord uses almost the same mysterious words, this time saying, "He that *loveth his life loseth it*; and he that *hateth his life* in this world shall keep it unto life eternal" (John 12:25).

We have been content with renouncing our sins and keeping ourselves! We have failed to see that *"himself"* in a man may stand as completely in the way of the Holy Spirit as one's sins, and still more we have failed to see that the life which flows in us from the source of the first Adam may hinder the manifestation of the life of Jesus in our mortal flesh. But what is this *life* which a man may seek to save and in so doing *lose*? What *life* is this which we are disposed to love instead of hate, and thereby suffer eternal loss?

The margin of the A.S.V. gives the word *"soul"* for life in every passage we have referred to, and Paul in his first letter to the Corinthians throws light upon this when he writes, "The first man Adam became a *living soul.* The last Adam became a *life-giving Spirit.*" "The first man is of the earth, earthy. The second Man is of heaven" (1 Corinthians 15:45, 47).

The life we are called to renounce, or hate, is the life which we receive from the first Adam. We may call it the soulish life to distinguish it from the heavenly life, which is given to us in union with the Lord from heaven. In another place the Lord describes it as a man's "*own* life"; therefore he loves it, for it is part of himself. We also love the soulish life because it works in the *realm of the senses* or *consciousness,* and has more affinity with the things of earth. The emotional, sensuous life is largely mingled with the true life from God in the early days of the child of God; hence the changing moods and "up and down" experiences of many, even when not convicted of definite disobedience or of yielding to any known sin. But to live in the Spirit, walk in the Spirit, and depend alone upon Him who is a life-giving Spirit, brings us into a realm of changeless peace infinitely beyond the pleasant emotions of the senses and the changing joys of earth.

It is the work of the Holy Spirit to wield the sword of the Spirit, the Word of God, and divide within us all that is soulish (Hebrews

4:12) from all that is true spirit. As the Word dwells in us richly and the dividing takes place, it is for us to *hate the soul-life revealed* and "lose" it by yielding it to the cross.

If we would follow the Lamb and have His life manifested through us so that we truly walk in His steps in the midst of men, we must know the *depth of His cross*; and if we would enter into all the benefits of His death, we must on our part *deny, renounce, hate,* all our "own" to take of His.

How far and how deep the renouncing goes determines how far and deep we know the power of His resurrection. We renounce our sins that we may die with Christ to those sins; we renounce the world and so die with Christ to the world; we renounce "I myself" and thereby give way to Christ Himself to reign within. And in like manner we renounce the soulish life *from which springs all the activities of the life on earth,* and "always bearing about in the body the dying of Jesus" we learn to draw upon the life of Jesus—that it may be manifested in our mortal flesh and, through us, quicken souls around.

THE CROSS AND TIES OF EARTH

> "He that loveth father or mother . . . son or daughter, more than Me is *not worthy of Me.* And he that doth not take his cross and follow after Me is *not worthy of Me.* He that findeth his life shall lose it; and he that loseth his life for My sake shall find it."—Matthew 10:37–39.

Here we have a glimpse into one of the many aspects of what taking the cross involves and what renouncing the soul-life means.

The soulish life may be bound up in strong earth ties: lawful ties, yet held so tenaciously that they need the death of the cross and the deep working of the Holy Spirit to bring them to their right place "in the Lord." The keenest sword-work God has to do is the separating of soul and spirit in the relationships of earth, for the path of following the Lamb is scarcely possible without a point, sometime or other, where the claims of the Crucified One clash with ties of love. Then it is that "a man's foes" are "they of his own household," and loved hands are the ones that nail us to the cross. Then it is that the master whispers, "*He that loveth*" loved ones "*more than Me is not worthy of Me*," and the obedient heart, with many tears, consents to follow the Lord, laying at His feet that wherein its life was bound; and losing all for *His* dear sake, finds *all given back,* transfigured by the joy of heaven.

Was it no suffering to the Lord Himself when His kinsmen said He was beside Himself, and when they did not understand the necessity laid upon Him to fulfill His heavenly Father's will? He could do nothing other than obey the heavenly vision, although it meant a path contrary to the hopes of His friends.

Thus must it be with every follower of the Lamb. But also with every step—*if taken assuredly in obedience to God*—the outcome will be as with the Pattern; for the day did come when His brethren believed on Him, and His word was fulfilled in His own case: "He that loseth . . . *findeth.*"

THE CROSS AND CONFESSION OF CHRIST

> "Take up his cross. . . . For whosoever shall lose his life [soul] for My sake *and the gospel's* shall save it."—Mark 8:34–35.

The context of these words indicates that the soul-life may be strongly centered in a love of popularity and fear of men which would make the believer *ashamed* of Christ and of His words in a time when the sinful generation around oppose Him and the truth He spoke from the Father.

"Whosoever shall be ashamed of Me and of *My words* . . . the Son of Man also shall be ashamed of him, when He cometh in the glory of His Father" (Mark 8:38), said the Lord in connection with His call to the cross as recorded by Mark, when He spoke of losing one's life for His sake *and the gospel's.* For nothing but taking the cross of Christ—renouncing "I myself" and the soulish life of earth—can so sever us from the world that we are not ashamed to be outside the camp, bearing His reproach.

The Lord knew beforehand the "offense of the cross" and the offense of the *message* of the cross, for the gospel as revealed to Paul is the "word of the cross." To preach Jesus Christ as a "pattern Man" is no cross, for His Sermon on the Mount is admitted by the natural man to be unsurpassed by the words of any teacher ever known on earth. The arch-deceiver of men will even encourage men to "copy the life" described by the Sermon on the Mount if they will but *leave out the cross* and the scorned Christ as the enabling power. Yea, even more, the devil will give the power to outwardly, and seemingly, obey the laws of the kingdom if thereby he can delude the soul into accepting a gospel that omits the atoning cross of Jesus Christ.

To preach a gospel of the Christ and His *cross*—with peace coming only through the *blood* of the cross, and a cross that speaks of *separation from the world* and claims an *absolute entire surrender to the Man of Calvary*—will mean in truth a losing, a renouncing, of the soul-life; for in preaching such a gospel as this, the soulish life with its love for the glory of men is lost for the sake of the Christ and His gospel.

THE CROSS DAILY

> "Let him *deny himself* and take up his cross *daily* . . . for whosoever would save his life [soul] shall lose it."—Luke 9:23–24.

Just as the apostle Paul said, "*always* bearing about in the body the dying of Jesus," so the Lord said, "*daily*."

We have seen in the writings of Paul that there is a union with Christ's death which admits us into a new sphere of life, from which we look back upon the cross as a gulf fixed between us and the past; and we have seen also a *continuous* conformity to the death of Christ, which is a necessary condition for the ever-increasing manifestation of the power of the resurrection in reality.

In harmony with this after-revealed gospel to Paul, the Lord Christ bids His followers take the cross *daily*. *Daily* we must definitely account that we are crucified with Christ and arm ourselves with the mind of the crucified Jesus—becoming obedient unto death. *Daily* must there be the deliberate losing of the soulish life that we may exchange it for the life of the Lord Himself. *Daily* we must be willing to be led into fuller conformity to His death, not making for ourselves a cross but quickly yielding to "the cross in the way."

Daily! Daily! Daily! the Lord calls to the cross, if His children are truly to be His crucified messengers to a needy world.

THE CROSS AND ITS CLAIMS

> "If any man cometh unto Me, and hateth not his own father . . . mother . . . wife . . . children . . . brethren . . . sisters, yea, and his *own life* also, he CANNOT be My disciple. . . . Whoso-ever doth not bear his *own* cross . . . CANNOT be My disciple. . . . Whosoever he be of you that RE-NOUNCETH NOT all that he hath, he cannot be My disciple."—Luke 14:26–27, 33.

Unconditional surrender is the keynote of this entire passage, for the absolute claim of God, as Creator and Redeemer, upon all that we are and have is graphically put forth by the Creator-Redeemer Himself.

Every word is significant and unqualified. Father, mother, wife, children, brothers and sisters, must each and all be yielded to the Redeemer, henceforth to be held *in the Lord* and for the Lord alone; and not only so, but the Redeemer claims the very *life* of the one He redeems, for the believer owes his *life* unto his Lord—he is not his own!

Neither may he leave the cross to the Christ and think that *he* can escape it. He must bear his *own* cross—i.e., the cross of Jesus as it affects his *own* life—and follow the Lord in

His path of the cross all the way. Moreover, the taking of the cross will without doubt lead him into places where he will learn that he has no resources in himself, and he will be compelled to "*renounce all that he hath*" (Luke 14:33) as of no avail to meet the forces brought against him by the terrible foe.

"Renounce all that he hath" seems to be the summing up of the claims of the cross, the holocaust by which Christ purchased His redeemed. But let us not forget that the believer "renounces" his all only to be given "a hundredfold, *now in this time*," and "in the age to come *eternal* life" (Mark 10:29–30, mg.).

In brief, we deny—or renounce—*ourselves* or else we deny the Lord who bought us. But if we have had the cross of Jesus unveiled to us in the power of the Spirit, our "own cross" will be lost sight of in *His*. We shall joyfully reckon that the sufferings of this present time are not worthy to be compared with the glory which shall be revealed in us by and by!

The call to the cross is imperative; the claims of the cross are unqualified; the glory of the cross unspeakable! Shall we not heed the call?

CHAPTER 13

"Hath the stumbling-block of the cross been done away?"

—Galatians 5:11.

THE PREACHING OF THE CROSS

"I determined not to know anything among you save Jesus Christ, and Him crucified."

—1 Corinthians 2:2.

THERE is a Spirit-given unveiling of Calvary and all that it meant to the Son of God and to a dying world which creates in the believer a *passion* begotten of the cross—a passion as a burning fire (Jeremiah 20:9) in the heart. It kindles an intense desire that the Man of Calvary should see of the travail of His soul and be satisfied, a desire that becomes the dominating power of the life and swallows up, so to speak, all *personal thought* of sacrifice or gain.

Such a passion is revealed in the life and words of the apostle Paul and is strikingly emphasized in his letter to the Corinthians when he writes that he *determined* to know nothing among them save "Jesus Christ and Him crucified."

What a complete self-effacement this determination meant to him we little understand today, for Christianity has *glorified* the cross. In Paul's time the cross was the "instrument of punishment of the vilest malefactors; it was associated with all that was most odious, contemptible and horrible . . . just as the word *gibbet* now" (Conybeare's note).

Truly it took a revelation from God to make a haughty Pharisee glory in the cross and not to be ashamed of such a strange gospel. *A criminal's gibbet the place of the world's salvation!* No wonder they called him mad.

Nevertheless "I *determined*," he writes to the Corinthians, "not to know anything among you save Jesus Christ—*and Him crucified*."

Corinth was highly cultured in intellect but dissolute in morals. It was occupied with philosophy and literature, but it was sunk in sin. Should he adapt his message to the Corinthians and win a hearing for the gospel by making use of human wisdom and knowledge? This must have been the question in the mind of Paul as he pondered over the condition of Corinth and its people.

The apostle might well have determined to meet the Corinthians with weapons of man's wisdom, for he had studied secular learning at Tarsus—by some considered a better school than Athens—and had been trained in all the Hebrew law in Jerusalem. Added to this, he was a Roman citizen and could have taken a position of authority and met the cultured Corinthians on their own ground in every point, had he so desired.

Moreover he knew—the sensitive, clear-sighted man *knew*—all that they would say if he failed to take that reasonable approach. The message of the cross would be considered rank folly and he himself be counted but a *fool*!

The apostle foresees it all, and *in the face of all* deliberately elects to put aside reliance upon weapons of the flesh and determines to proclaim the obnoxious message of a crucified Messiah, casting himself entirely upon the Holy Spirit to make "the word of the cross" the power of God, so that all who believed would have their faith anchored not upon "persuasive [or *enticing*] words of man's wisdom" (1 Corinthians 2:4) but on the power of God alone.

This decision of the apostle shows us how absolutely he sinks himself for his message! How wholly he casts aside all personal self-glory! Such messengers of the cross are needed today, for in our century we find ourselves face to face with almost the same conditions as met the apostle in cultured Corinth; and God's messengers have still to determine whether they will rely on carnal weapons and on "*words which man's wisdom teaches,*" or cast themselves on the power of God to bear witness to the message of the cross—a message still as obnoxious to the natural man as in the days of Paul.

THE PREACHING OF THE CROSS

> "And I, brethren, . . . came not with excellency of speech or of wisdom. . . . My speech and my preaching were not in persuasive words of wisdom."—1 Corinthians 2:1–4.

The apostle had been describing God's instruments for the fulfillment of His purposes in the world: foolish, weak, base, despised things, chosen to put to shame the wise and strong: yea, even "*things that are not*," chosen by God to "*bring to nought the things that are*"!

"And I, brethren," writes the apostle—*I* came thus to you with no "enticing words," no "persuasive words of wisdom." As one whom men despised, "I was with you in weakness, and in fear, and in much trembling," proclaiming the mystery of God; and to my message was given the witness of God in the "*demonstration of the Spirit and of power*."

Unless the proclamation of the cross is borne witness to by the Holy Spirit it may easily become a stumbling-block, for without the illuminating and convincing power of the Spirit behind the message, carnal reason may reject it to turn to "another gospel which is not another"; or the mental light about the cross may serve as an opiate of conscience, and blinded ones may even materialize the message and adore the outward symbol of the cross and rest on an exterior form. For the adversary of the cross knows well that he can hold souls in his servitude under cover of the "sign of the cross" unless they have learned the true meaning of the cross by the power of the Holy Spirit.

Moreover, the "word of the cross" does not require persuasive words of man's wisdom for the manifestation of its power. The apostle goes so far as to say that "wisdom of words" makes the cross "of none effect" (1 Corinthians 1:17, A.V.)!

Does this explain the existence of so much knowledge about the death of Christ *without vital changes in the lives of men*?

Can the cross be made *void by the preacher*? How awful the thought! The God-Man pours out His soul unto death for the eternal salvation of men and his *messengers* make the cross of "none effect"! God forbid!

But how can the cross be "made void" by the "wisdom of words" of the preacher? It must be because "words which man's wisdom teaches" are definitely possible if the minister is occupied with his words rather than with the death of Him who died; for "wisdom of words" will surely draw attention to the messenger rather than to the *message*, to the oratory rather than to the *theme*, to the servant rather than to the *Master*.

Reverently may we not say that the message of Calvary must be the most sacred theme to God the Father, and He will not give one shade of glory to men in the proclaiming of the death of His Son.

The story of Calvary must be preached to a dying world in all its tragic *awfulness*, and "flowers of speech" as ill become the message as flowers around the cross if they had been strewn by those who watched the God-Man die. Moreover, the theme of the cross will not lend itself to rhetoric or poetic fancy. In brief, there is no place in the cross, either in its reality or its proclamation, for glory to the flesh.

In Paul, as an object lesson, we see what conditions are necessary for the effectual preaching of the cross. The message of Calvary must be proclaimed by those who are willing to be *crucified by the very preaching of the crucifixion of the Lord.*

The cross must be preached by those who know its power if it is to have the witness of the Holy Spirit and if the "word of the cross" is to be the energy of God to men. How the *Spirit* bore witness to the proclamation of the death and the resurrection of the Son of God we see in the Acts of the Apostles. The men who had stood by Calvary could preach Calvary. The men who had seen the risen Lord could witness to His resurrection. It was more than an historical fact to them, more than a doctrine or even a fundamental truth.

"I feel as if Christ died yesterday!" said Martin Luther. It is the special office of the Holy Spirit today to unveil the death of Christ to the messengers of the cross so that it becomes as real to them as it was to the apostles. Then He will be able to "placard" Christ crucified before the eyes of those to whom they are sent, and the passion begotten of the cross will cast out all thought of the praise or condemnation of men as with broken hearts the messengers proclaim the death of the Son of God as the only hope for dying men.

Thus it was revealed to Paul, until he could only cry, "Woe is unto me if I preach not the gospel." Beholding Calvary from the standpoint of God, and Him who for the joy set before Him "endured the cross, despising the shame," all pride is swept away, and he elects to preach the cross even though the cross he preaches thereby becomes his *own* cross, and he, like his Lord, becomes despised and rejected by men.

THE MESSAGE OF THE CROSS

> "The word of the cross . . . is the *power* of God."— 1 Corinthians 1:18.

The Greek word translated "power" in this passage is *dunamis*—the word from which we get the English word dynamite! The apostle declares that "the word of the cross" is the *dunamis*, or energy, of God. The expression signifies not *latent* power, but *power in action.* In the cross of Calvary, God has centered His power to deliver a lost and ruined world, and "*the word of the cross*" is God's "power in action" to all who receive it, for it has Omnipotence behind it. "I, if I be lifted up," said the Lord Jesus, "will draw all men unto Myself."

But it is "the word *of* the cross"—not words *about* the cross—that is the energy of

God. Not speculation as to what the cross means, but the pure and simple preaching of the cross of Christ as Paul preached it, taught by the risen Lord Himself.

The servants of God need to face the question today whether they really believe that divine energy is in the message of the cross, or do we limit God and think that "the word of the cross" needs many words to explain it? Is it not the key devised by the All-wise Creator to unlock the hearts of men? "It fits me as a key fits into a lock," said one; and this is true of every human heart, be he heathen or so-called Christian.

The message of the cross has Omnipotence behind it and in it, for it is the energy of God not only to the sinner burdened with his sins but "*unto us which are being saved.*" It meets the soul at every point of life, at every stage of spiritual growth, in every cry of need, and is never inappropriate or exhausted. *It is the power of God.*

ANTAGONISM TO THE CROSS

> "Many walk, of whom I told you often, and now tell you even weeping, that they are the

> enemies of the cross of Christ . . . who mind earthly things."—Philippians 3:18–19.

These words describe those in whom the proclamation of the message of Calvary will arouse active antagonism so that they become its enemies. We must be ever aware that enmity to the cross really has its origin in the love of all that the cross proclaims deliverance from! They who love *earthly* things resent a message which offers deliverance from the things they love!

It is true that the intellect is stumbled by the cross; yet the antagonism to the cross is mainly *moral,* both in the sinner and in the saved, for its message is only welcomed by those who desire freedom from the bondage of their sins and who hunger and thirst after the righteousness of God.

Enemies of the cross! The minister aiming at "*wisdom of words*" makes the cross *void* as he proclaims it; those who cling to external things find it an "*offense*" in its message of freedom from the elements of the world; and those who love the things of earth are called its "*enemies,*" for by their lives they place themselves in direct opposition to the very purpose of the cross. Oh solemn fact! Oh terrible thought! An *enemy* to Him who died to save me from myself, maybe while professedly His friend, perhaps while even a *messenger* of the cross—making void the message, not only by seeking glory for self in "wisdom of words" but by love of earthly things; for all self-indulgence is actually *enmity* to the cross of Christ.

THE RENEWING OF THE CROSS

> "They crucify to themselves the Son of God afresh, and put Him to an open shame."—Hebrews 6:6.

Apart from the context of this passage, it is sufficient for us to notice the solemn words which declare that the Son of God *can be crucified afresh,* and this time by those whom He has redeemed and who have tasted of the life He came to give to all who obey His call.

The Christ has passed beyond the power of the world and of the devil, and now only the blood-bought ones can re-crucify the Lamb. This is said of them when—having partaken of the Holy Spirit—they do despite to the Spirit of grace and choose to turn back to the "defilements of the world" from which they have escaped, and thus put the Lord who bought them to "open shame."

The warning comes in this passage of the Scripture about *the responsibility of light.* The apostle Peter solemnly says it is better not to have known the way of righteousness than to turn from the holy commandment delivered (2 Peter 2:20–21).

Oh that the Holy Spirit may so illumine the death on the cross to every child of God that the exceeding sinfulness of sin may be seen in the light of Calvary, and a *resisting of sin, even unto death,* be the mark of all the redeemed in these latter days, with the deep sense that, for those whom He has purchased with His own blood, all yielding to sin now is a "re-crucifixion, a re-binding, re-nailing, re-torturing, re-agonizing and re-killing" (Dean Vaughan) of the Son of God, who "suffered for sins once, the Righteous for the unrighteous, that He might bring us to God" (1 Peter 3:18).

"And one shall say unto Him, What are these wounds between Thine hands? Then He shall answer, Those with which I was wounded in the house of my friends" (Zechariah 13:6, mg.).

Oh child of God, beware of the *deceitfulness* of sin. Take heed that you do not presume on the grace of God by yielding to the least temptation with the thought that you can be freely forgiven. See, too, that you do not call sin by the name of "*infirmity*," nor in any degree excuse yourself for failure. Since Christ has died there is full victory for you, but you must walk in godly fear before the Lord and touch not anything that is *to you* the unclean thing.

CHAPTER 14

"By His own blood He entered in . . . having obtained eternal redemption for us."

—Hebrews 9:12.

THE LAMB IN THE MIDST OF THE THRONE

"Behold a door opened in heaven. . . ." "I saw in the midst of the throne . . . a Lamb standing, as though it had been slain."

—Revelation 4:1, 5:6.

IN the Apocalypse we have an account, in panoramic form, of the "coming" or "appearing" of the Lord Jesus Christ in that day when He shall be revealed from heaven with the angels of His power, dealing in solemn judgment with all who have "obeyed not the gospel."

In the opening words of the book we are told that the revelation was given by God to

His Son Jesus Christ for the express purpose of showing unto His servants "the things which must shortly come to pass," and that "He sent and signified them . . . unto His servant John" (Revelation 1:1).

The glorified Lord interpreted His cross to Paul that he might proclaim it as God's message of *love* to a dying world; but now He appears to the apostle John and charges him to write all that *he* is shown. In this unveiling given to him we have vividly brought before us the *heavenly* view of Calvary, and the eternal consequences of *rejecting* the Lamb of God who died on the cross to bear away the sins of the world.

The apostle, addressing the "seven churches" in the name of the Triune God, speaks of the Lord Jesus Christ as the "Firstborn of the dead," taking us back to Calvary at the very beginning of his message. Those to whom John is writing are the loved ones of Jesus, loved and "loosed" from their sins by His own blood shed on the cross (Revelation 1:4–6); but He rose from the dead, the Firstborn of many brethren, and entered heaven as their forerunner within the veil. He is there as the representative of His redeemed ones, who through His death for them, and their death with Him, are called out of the race of the first Adam and are now of the royal race of heaven, "kings and priests unto God," heirs of God and joint-heirs with Christ.

The apostle John then describes his meeting with the glorified Man of Calvary when he was given the messages which he is about to transmit to the churches at the Lord's command. As he falls at the feet of Him whose eyes are as a flame of fire, he hears the voice he once knew so well on earth, saying, "*Fear not; I am . . . the Living One; I became dead, and behold, I am alive for evermore*" (Revelation 1:17–18, mg.).

This *glorious* Christ is the very same Jesus whom the apostle had seen upon the cross of shame. The very hand that was pierced now touches him. The very body he had seen in the upper room at Jerusalem, when the risen Lord showed His disciples His hands and His side, is the same in the glory. His disciples had seen Him go up into heaven, but now heaven is opened and He who became dead is shown to be alive for evermore, with the keys of *death* and of *Hades* in His power.

In the messages which follow, given to the apostle for the churches, the Lord describes Himself tenderly to those in tribulation as He "who *became dead*, and *lived again*" (Revelation 2:8, mg.). As the One who had suffered, and triumphed in suffering, He bids them be "faithful unto death" that they also might receive their crown.

In the messages addressed to those He "purchased with his own blood" a veil is again drawn over the glorious Lord. But then "a door" is "opened in heaven" (Revelation 4:1). The apostle is taken up "in the Spirit" to the very heart of heaven, strengthened by the touch of the pierced hand of the Man of Calvary, to behold Him who only hath immortality, dwelling in light unapproachable! He sees the throne of "the Lord God, the Almighty," hears the "lightnings and voices and thunders proceeding out of the throne," and beholds the worship which day and night surrounds the throne of Him as Creator and Lord of all! The heavenly beings keep saying, "Holy, holy, holy is the Lord God, the Almighty. . . . Thou didst *create all things*, and because of Thy will they were created" (Revelation 4:8–11).

In the hand of the Lord God the Creator is seen a "book." The cup of iniquity on earth is full to the brim. The Creator has determined that the fullness of time has come when the dispensation of grace must close and the era of *judgment* upon rebellious man must open.

A proclamation is sounded throughout heaven, "Who is worthy to open the book?" Who is worthy to execute the eternal purposes of Him before whom angels veil their faces and cry, "Holy, holy, holy is the Lord of Hosts"? Not one is found worthy in heaven, not even the highest archangel of God.

Then who shall open the book? To whom will the Most High God commit the solemn trust of dealing with a rebellious world, since no archangel in heaven is worthy?

And suddenly John beholds in the very midst of the throne of God Himself "a *Lamb* standing, as though it had been slain" (Revelation 5:6)!

The Father "hath given all judgment unto the Son: that all may honor the Son, even as they honor the Father" (John 5:22–23). Only He who of His own accord laid down His life as a ransom for sinners is worthy, or *fitted*, to execute the judgment inevitable for all who "obey not the gospel" (2 Thessalonians 1:8–9).

The Lamb standing in the midst of the throne is said to be "*as though it had been slain*." The sacrifice made on Calvary's cross is, as it were, ever fresh and new, enshrined in the heart of heaven and vividly kept before the eyes of all the company of heaven.

The Lamb had "seven horns, and seven eyes, which are the seven Spirits of God, sent forth into all the earth" (Revelation 5:6). In the vision of the Creator's throne (4:5) the "seven Spirits" are seen as "before the throne," but it has pleased the Father that in His *Christ* should "all the fullness dwell"—"all the fullness of the Godhead bodily." Consequently in the Lamb slain, as seen enthroned in heaven, is centered the fullness of the Holy Spirit, fullness of *power*, fullness of *light* and *vision*; and out of the slain Lamb, the Holy Spirit is "*sent forth into all the earth*," for He is ever proceeding from the Father, through the Son, into the world of men, seeking to enter hearts which turn to Calvary in self-despair and loathing of sin. He is ready to apply to each the power of the death of the Son of

God, and to possess each redeemed one on behalf of Him who purchased them with His own precious blood.

THE LAMB IN JUDGMENT

> "And He came and took the book."—Revelation 5:7, A.V.

He—the One who had died on behalf of sinful men—*He* took the book into His own pierced hand, knowing all that it meant to those He had yearned to save.

And the redeemed in heaven, gazing upon Him coming forth again as the Lamb to fulfill His Father's will, sang—

> "Thou art *worthy* to take the Book . . . for Thou wast slain, and hast redeemed us to God by Thy blood, out of every kindred, and tongue, and people, and nation."—Revelation 5:9, A.V.

And angels, ten thousand times ten thousand, took up the strain, saying, "*Worthy* is the Lamb that hath been slain," while every created thing was heard saying, "Unto Him that sitteth on the throne, and unto the Lamb, be the blessing, and the honor, and the glory, and the dominion, forever and ever"!

In this opening of the heavens to the apostle John we see Calvary from the *heavenly* standpoint.

The Lamb slain on earth is *enthroned* in heaven!

The Crucified One is the *Glorified One*! He is glorified as the Lamb of Calvary, and as the Lamb *all the worship of heaven* centers around Him.

All that is now unveiled of His work in heaven shows that all is based on His sacrifice upon the cross. He is in heaven as the Conqueror from Calvary; and as the Lamb who prevailed on the cross it is given to Him to open each seal preceding the awful judgments on the world which rejects Him. The Father commits all judgment into the hands of Him who became the propitiation for the sins of the world!

From this we see something of the unspeakable heinousness of sin in the sight of the Holy God, and especially of the greater sin of rejecting or neglecting the sacrifice provided by God for the sins of the people. That the Lamb, who loved the sinner and died in his behalf, who suffered unparalleled sorrow and shame in giving His life as a ransom for many, should now have to open *the era of judgment* upon the sinful world shows the impossibility of sin being passed over by our righteous God. The Christ, by offering His life for sinners, obtained a "day of grace" for the sin-blighted earth, but now it is *over*, and He must abolish all contrary "rule, and all authority and power." "And when all things shall be subdued unto Him," then shall He deliver up the Kingdom to God, even the Father (see 1 Corinthians 15:24–28, A.V.).

As the judgments fall, the terror-stricken souls on earth need none to tell them that the *essence* of their sin has been the rejection of the crucified Lamb of God, for they instinctively cry to the mountains and the rocks to be hidden not only from their Creator but from "*the wrath of the Lamb.*"

Ah, who shall fathom the depth of the wrath of wounded love! The wrath of despised and rejected mercy?

THE LAMB AS LEADER

> "The Lamb that is in the midst of the throne . . . shall guide them."—Revelation 7:17.

The Lamb slain on earth and enthroned in heaven is not only the center of heaven's worship and the opener of the seals of judgments upon the earth, but we are given glimpse after glimpse of the Lamb as the *Leader* in heaven of the various companies of those He has redeemed from among men.

The terror-stricken on earth know that they have wounded the Lamb, but the redeemed in heaven know that they are there *because* of Him.

The first group of the redeemed, pictured in the "living creatures and the elders," do not hesitate to own that they have been "purchased unto God" (Revelation 5:8–9) with the blood of the Lamb, as they watch Him take the book and open the first six seals.

Later we come upon another company described as "a great multitude, which no man could number," gathered "out of every nation, and of all tribes and peoples and tongues" (see Revelation 7:9–17). "They stand *before the throne of God,*" and are said to "serve Him day and night." And He who sits on the throne spreads over them His "tabernacle," or the covering of His manifested

Presence. These are those who have "washed their robes" in the blood of the Lamb. And He who for the joy set before Him endured the cross, Himself becomes their Shepherd, to lead them on unto ever-fresh fountains of water of life. Their sufferings are over, and God Himself wipes all tears from their eyes.

Once more we see the Lamb standing at the head of another company, this time a definite number (Revelation 14:1–4). They are also described as those who have been "purchased *out of* the earth," "*purchased from among men*." And they "follow the Lamb whithersoever He goeth."

THE LAMB AS WARRIOR

> "These shall war against the Lamb, and the Lamb shall overcome them."—Revelation 17:14.

Judgment after judgment has fallen upon the earth as the seals have been opened and the trumpets of woe sounded! The iniquity has waxed worse and worse, until even in heaven a voice from the four horns of the golden altar has cried to God for vengeance (Revelation 9:13–14).

"The horns of the golden altar, in the Old Testament type, received the blood of the sacrifice offered on the brazen altar, and from the golden horns the voice of blood cried to God to *spare*, but now the voice cries for the letting loose of the powers of judgment.

"The implication is that [on earth] God's appointed way of forgiveness has been set aside; that the divine system of gracious atonement, and salvation, has been rejected. Mankind in their guilt have blasphemously pronounced against God's plan of reconciliation, and the wickedness of earth has risen so high, especially in point of *antagonism to the cross* . . . that the altar itself, which otherwise cries only for mercy, is forced into a cry of vengeance" (Sciss).

Picture after picture of the terrible doings of rebellious men, working as instruments of the satanic powers, follow, with glimpses of some who come "victorious" out of the sinful strife, until again we see the lamb as *Leader*, and this time of a host of warriors. The "abominations of the earth" have culminated in the mystery of Babylon the Great, drunken with the blood of the saints. The rebellion of the powers on earth seems to have come to a head, and is focused now "*against the Lamb*." But the Lamb who was slain on the cross is "Lord of Lords and King of Kings"! As the Conqueror from Calvary, He is sure of victory, and the *warriors* who *are with Him in the last great warfare* are those whom He has specially "called" and "chosen," and who are "*faithful*" (Revelation 17:14).

After this final conflict between the Lamb and all that is against God and His Anointed, the voice of a great multitude in heaven, as the roar of many waters, is heard saying—

> "The Lord our God, the Almighty, reigneth. Let us rejoice and be exceeding glad, and let us give the glory unto Him: for the marriage of the Lamb is come."—Revelation 19:6–7.

The Christ who conquered on the cross, and waited while His purchased ones were being called out of all nations, has now finally triumphed and put down all authority and power under His feet.

The hour is drawing nigh when the supreme purpose for which Christ Jesus gave His life is to be fulfilled. For He "loved the

Church and gave Himself up for it . . . that He might present the Church to Himself a *glorious* Church, not having spot or wrinkle, or any such thing" (Ephesians 5:25–27). Now it is "given unto her that she should array herself in fine linen, bright and pure, for the fine linen is the righteous acts of the saints" (Revelation 19:8).

Once more the heaven opens (Revelation 19:11–12), and there comes forth the Man of Calvary with eyes as a "flame of fire," and the armies following Him are clothed in fine linen, white and pure. He comes forth to take final possession of the conquered earth, over which He now must reign. The devil is bound for the thousand years, and the kingdoms of this world become the kingdoms of our Lord and of His Christ; and they who are the king-priests, redeemed from among men, "reign with Him the thousand years" (Revelation 20:1–6).

After these things the apostle gazes on into eternity, beyond the Judgment of the Great White Throne and the destruction of the last enemy—death. He is shown in vision the Bride-City coming down from God, "made ready as a bride adorned for her husband" (Revelation 21:2). The first heaven and the first earth have passed away! He who sits on the throne says, "Behold, I make all things new," and now "they are come to pass." Shall Calvary be forgotten? No! The name of Him who became dead, and lived again, is still

THE LAMB

All other names revealing various aspects of Christ are now not needed in the full vision of His glory. They are merged in this name which is above every name—the name which unto the "ages of the ages" will keep ever fresh and clear before the company of heaven that *marvelous* hour in the annals of time when the Only Begotten of the Father visited the earth, and on a cross laid down His life for those whose light is now "clear as crystal" and who shine as the sun in the kingdom of their Father.

The names of the chosen apostles who continued with Him in His temptations on earth are engraved on the "foundations" of the Bride-City, for they laid the foundation of the Church as they proclaimed the word of the cross in the face of the scorn and rebellion of men. None are in the Bride-City save those whose names are written "*in the book of life of the Lamb that hath been slain from the foundation of the world*" (Revelation 13:8 and 21:27)—they who gloried in His cross and, accepting life through His *death*, were conformed to the image of the Lamb.

ENDNOTES

1. If Paul had been present at the tragedy of Golgotha, surely he would have made some reference to it in his writings.
2. "The sense of feebleness, or prostration, to which man is reduced by the working of the law," is "the process of dying in fact."—Lightfoot.

Other Books by Jessie Penn-Lewis

All Things New
The Awakening in Wales
The Battle for the Mind
The Centrality of the Cross
The Climax of the Risen Life
Communion with God
The Conquest of Canaan
The Cross: The Touchstone of Faith
Dying to Live
Face to Face
Fruitful Living
Life in the Spirit
Power for Service
Soul and Spirit
Spiritual Warfare
Thy Hidden Ones
The Warfare with Satan
War on the Saints
The Work of the Holy Spirit

CLC PUBLICATIONS
Fort Washington, PA 19034

This book is published by CLC Publications, an outreach of CLC Ministries International. The purpose of CLC is to make evangelical Christian literature available to all nations so that people may come to faith and maturity in the Lord Jesus Christ. We hope this book has been life changing and has enriched your walk with God through the work of the Holy Spirit. If you would like to know more about CLC, we invite you to visit our website:

www.clcusa.org

To know more about the remarkable story of the founding of CLC International we encourage you to read

LEAP OF FAITH

Norman Grubb

Paperback
Size $5^{1}/_{4}$ x 8, Pages 248
ISBN: 978-0-87508-650-7
ISBN (*e-book*): 978-1-61958-055-8

THE WARFARE WITH SATAN

Jessie Penn-Lewis

A series of addresses on spiritual conflict, particularly for those who have been brought by the Holy Spirit into the experience of union with Christ in the heavenly places.

Paperback
Size 4 ¼ x 7, Pages 157
ISBN: 978-1-61958-255-2
ISBN (*e-book*): 978-1-61958-256-9

THE WORK OF THE HOLY SPIRIT

Jessie Penn-Lewis

In this short book, Jessie Penn-Lewis outlines the ministry of the Holy Spirit to us as comforter, teacher, and witness to Christ.

Paperback
Size 4 ¼ x 7, Pages 63
ISBN: 978-0-87508-961-4